Mental Health Matters

Mental Health Matters

A practical guide to identifying and understanding mental health issues in primary schools

by Paula Nagel

BLOOMSBURY

LONDON · OXFORD · NEW YORK · NEW DELHI · SYDNEY

Bloomsbury Education

An imprint of Bloomsbury Publishing Plc

50 Bedford Square   1385 Broadway
London   New York
WC1B 3DP   NY 10018
UK   USA

www.bloomsbury.com

Bloomsbury is a registered trademark of Bloomsbury Publishing Plc

First published 2016

© Paula Nagel, 2016

British Library Cataloguing-in-Publication Data
A catalogue record for this book is available from the British Library.

ISBN:
PB: 978-1-4729-2140-6
ePub: 978-1-4729-2476-6
ePDF: 978-1-4729-2141-3

Library of Congress Cataloging-in-Publication Data
A catalog record for this book is available from the Library of Congress.

10 9 8 7 6 5 4 3 2 1

Typeset by Newgen Knowledge Works (P) Ltd., Chennai, India
Printed and bound in India by Replika Press Pvt. Ltd.

Every reasonable effort has been made to trace copyright holders of material reproduced in this book, but if any have been inadvertently overlooked the publishers would be glad to hear from them.

This book is produced using paper that is made from wood grown in managed, sustainable forests. It is natural, renewable and recyclable. The logging and manufacturing processes conform to the environmental regulations of the country of origin.

To view more of our titles please visit **www.bloomsbury.com**

For Gary, Laura and Hannah

Contents

Introduction

Most teachers can think of a child whose behaviour doesn't respond to the usual strategies. When worrying or disruptive behaviour persists despite clear and consistent classroom management and support, it can be puzzling, frustrating and challenging, and a drain on energy as well as resources.

Sometimes, behaviour is described as loud and aggressive, and escalates without any obvious triggers. This externalised or 'acting out' behaviour demands our attention and can have an immediate and visible impact on the classroom atmosphere, relationships and curriculum delivery, not to mention stress levels! At other times, behaviour is described as a 'series of low level irritations' that don't seem particularly significant when viewed as isolated incidents, but over the course of a lesson, a morning, or a day can get under the skin and be exhausting for everyone concerned – both physically and emotionally.

For other children, their behaviour is less visible, with little immediate impact on daily classroom management. They might withdraw from interactions and appear passive and unmotivated. Some children may become increasingly anxious or nervous and fearful of trying new things. It can be easy for these children to slip under the radar, but this internalised or 'acting in' behaviour can be extremely debilitating.

In my work as an educational psychologist, many of the consultations with school staff have focused on children who display difficult, disturbing and puzzling behaviour as described above. In such cases, approaches that focus on sanctions and rewards to resolve the behaviour often don't get to the root of the problem. Therefore, an important part of any consultation is to take the time to reflect and be curious about the behaviour, to decide what we need to find out more about and who else needs to be involved. A key question underpinning these consultations is:

I wonder what this behaviour is trying to tell us?

The answer, for a significant number of children, is that their behaviour is telling us about an unmet or emerging mental health problem.

With this in mind, I have collated a series of sample case studies for this book. These are examples of typical consultations where behaviour has been better understood by recognising the risk factors for mental health problems and identifying the underlying or emerging mental health issues.

Using this book

This book is divided into six chapters.

Chapters 1 and 2 consider some of the risk factors linked to mental health problems, as well as exploring some of the protective factors for positive mental health. They draw attention to the importance of targeted support for those experiencing mental health problems, as well as universal approaches to promoting positive mental health and well-being for all.

Chapters 3–5 feature case study consultations which follow a series of steps to consider the link between mental health and behaviour. All of the case studies use the same framework of five steps that each pose a core question.

Five step framework

STEP 1. **What can we see?** The first step is to summarise concerns about the child's progress, starting with a description of their behaviour, and thinking about how often it occurs, how long it lasts and where it usually happens.

STEP 2. **What have we tried?** The second step is to reflect on the strategies and interventions that have already been tried in school, and the impact they have had.

STEP 3. **What do we know?** Next, we bring together everything we know about the child in order to consider the wider perspective; this includes incorporating the child's own views, the views of those who know them best such as their family, as well as looking at information held in school.

STEP 4. **What is the mental health message?** In this step, we reflect on what we understand about the child's difficulties, thinking about risk factors and warning signs, in order to consider whether there is a link between mental health and behaviour. Can we identify or predict any emerging mental health problems?

STEP 5. **What would personalised planning look like for this child?** Finally, in light of this understanding, we look at how we can best support the child. How can we strengthen protective factors for mental health and implement targeted mental health support?

At the end of each chapter you will find a quick 'At a Glance' summary of the main points covered for ease of reference.

Finally, Chapter 6 brings the book to a conclusion with a series of points to encourage reflection on the mental health priorities that matter in your school.

Using the case studies

The case studies in this book do not feature real children, but they are based on real-life consultations and illustrate some typical behavioural concerns shared by staff. Most of the children reflected in these case studies will continue to have their needs met within school through personalised approaches and pastoral and SEN support. For some children, the information gathered at this stage will support referral to other services.

The aims of the case studies are to enable us to reflect on:

- the link between mental health and behaviour
- the signs and the risk factors associated with emerging mental health problems
- practical strategies for early intervention and support.

In real life, the consultation questions were worked through over a series of sessions, enabling staff to gather information from parents, other members of staff and the child, before bringing the information together to think about the possible reasons underpinning the behaviour.

The case studies highlight some of the risk factors that can impact on mental health and behaviour. These risk factors can be:

- in the child (Chapter 3)
- in the family and environment (Chapter 4)
- linked to significant events (Chapter 5).

For ease of reference, the case studies have been placed under one of these risk factor headings, whilst acknowledging that risk factors are often overlapping and cumulative and rarely occur in isolation. Indeed, within these case studies there is often a combination of several risk factors that impact on behaviour. The 'Five step framework' that follows in each case study invites us to be curious about all the risk factors that may be present. It is important to remember that the presence of risk factors per se does not necessarily lead to mental health problems. Children can, and do, respond in very different ways to challenge and adversity. However, awareness of these risk factors, as well as awareness of the signs that can indicate emerging mental health problems, can help inform early identification and support.

Although you may recognise the behaviour of some of your children in these case studies, the reasons underpinning the behaviour may vary. Children can present with similar behaviour yet their unmet needs may be very different. For this reason, these case studies are not intended to be diagnostic but to demonstrate a framework to help us consider the unmet needs that might be behind the behaviour.

While we know that not all behaviour difficulties are linked to mental health problems, the 'Five step framework' reminds us to consider a mental health perspective when trying to understand the message behind the behaviour. This approach reflects the emphasis in the *Special Educational Needs and Disabilities (SEND) Code of Practice (2015)*, which replaced the previous category of 'behaviour, emotional and social development,' with 'social, emotional and mental health difficulties'. This encourages us to look beyond the behaviour to think about the possibility of unmet social, emotional and mental health needs and to shape responses and interventions accordingly.

Staff in schools are not mental health specialists nor should they be, but they do need to be able to spot the signs of mental distress and provide early support. In some cases, the provision of early support will help to further clarify the nature of a child's difficulties and help make the decision about seeking specialist help.

This book is *not about diagnosing mental health disorders and their treatment*. It is a resource for primary school staff, particularly newly qualified teachers and support staff, to raise awareness of children's mental health and promote confidence in identifying and supporting mental health problems. I hope this book will help you to understand and identify some of the potential triggers and risk factors for mental health problems in your school, highlight protective and early intervention strategies, and provide a useful framework for assessing the behaviour of those children who cause most concern – a framework which holds mental health at its core.

1 Understanding children's mental health

What is mental health?

Are you aware of your mental health? Do you acknowledge your mental health concerns in the same way as your physical aches and pains? Do you look after your worries and anxieties as you would a sore throat or a pulled muscle? And are you as likely to chat with family and friends about your mental health as you would about your physical health?

We all have mental health. It affects how we think, feel and behave. Yet the term 'mental health' is often misused and misunderstood. Often, when people hear the words 'mental health', they immediately think 'mental illness' or long-lasting, often severe, difficulties. But mental health is something that impacts on us all, even if we don't always acknowledge it. It is part of everyday life to face various stresses and strains; but we cope with these challenges will vary depending on a range of factors, including what else is going on in our lives at that time, our individual personality traits and learned coping strategies. Often, when faced with stress and challenge, this will be reflected in a change in our behaviour, whether that be hiding away or hitting out! Although a change in behaviour can be a typical short term response, when we have positive mental health we are better equipped to draw on resources that will help us to navigate through adversity.

Having positive mental health doesn't mean a life free from challenge or upset, but it can act like a buffer to help us manage what life throws at us. When we have good mental health we are more likely to be able to handle stress, get on better with others and make choices. So, our mental health needs to hold the same importance as our physical health, and awareness of this importance seems to be slowly shifting.

According to the *Attitudes to mental illness research report, (2014)* attitudes towards mental illness have become more positive, suggesting greater tolerance and understanding of mental health issues. For example, more people agree that, 'mental illness is an illness like any other,' and express inclusive attitudes towards people with a mental health illness. However, we still have some way to go. In a research report, *What is the impact of mental health-related stigma on help-seeking? (2014)* findings suggest that ongoing stigma surrounding mental health continues to impact on people's willingness to seek help for mental health problems.

It seems, therefore, that we are still some way from thinking about our mental health in the same way as our physical health. We expect our physical health to change over time and are often quick to identify these changes and do things to promote recovery, e.g. rest, exercise, change our diet, take medication. . . and if this doesn't work, we know where to go for support. Our physical health concerns are often the topic of many conversations. We might moan about our aches and pains, compare our symptoms and share what makes them better or worse. We show interest in others' physical health and often identify with their worries. Can we honestly say the same about our mental health?

It's time to put mental health on the same footing as our physical health. Just like our physical health, we need to know what good mental health looks like, what helps us to remain mentally healthy, and the signs that indicate it needs some attention. Furthermore, this mental health awareness needs to start with our children. Can we recognise when emotional responses are part and parcel of childhood development, and when they are signalling that a child is at risk of mental health problems? And if so, do we know what to do about it?

True or false?

Consider the following statements and decide which ones you think are true or false.

1. 'One in ten children and young people (ten percent) aged 5–16 have a clinically diagnosable mental health disorder.'
2. 'Many adults are not confident in being able to spot the signs of poor mental health in children'.
3. 'Children with learning disabilities are at much greater risk of having mental health problems than children who do not have learning disabilities.'
4. 'Half of all lifetime cases of diagnosable mental illness begin by age 14.'
5. 'The most important predictor of adult life satisfaction is emotional health, both in childhood and subsequently.'

Let's look at these statements in more detail.

1. 'One in ten children and young people (ten percent) aged 5–16 have a clinically diagnosable mental health disorder.'

This statement is TRUE and noted in the *Mental health of children and young people in Great Britain, 2004 summary report*. Therefore, according to this data, there could be on average, three children in every classroom with a diagnosable mental health disorder at any one time.

Some facts about childhood mental health disorders

- Sometimes mental health problems have such a long term and significant impact on functioning and behaviour that a mental health disorder is diagnosed.

- The three most common childhood mental health disorders are: emotional disorders, conduct disorders and hyperkinetic disorders (*Mental health of children and young people in Great Britain, 2004*).

- Emotional disorders include phobias, anxiety and depression. Sometimes emotional disorders present as physical symptoms, such as recurring sickness, stomach aches or headaches which have no physical explanation.

- Conduct disorders often present as defiant, troublesome and antisocial behaviour and can include verbal and physical aggression.

- Hyperkinetic disorders involve problems with inattention, impulsivity and over activity, and can include attention deficit hyperactivity disorder (ADHD).

- Some mental health diagnoses will be made for other disorders, including: autism spectrum disorder (ASD), tics, eating disorders and selective mutism.

- Disorders are more likely to occur when a child has been exposed to several risk factors, and are often diagnosed when a child has several co-occurring mental health problems.

- Only a mental health professional can diagnose disorders.

However, in addition to the one in ten with a diagnosable mental health disorder, there are likely to be several children in each classroom who have mental health 'problems' – children whose difficulties don't meet the criteria for diagnosis but nevertheless have mental health challenges that need to be recognised, understood and supported. The key for these children lies in recognising and supporting their emerging problems before they escalate into diagnosable disorders, and schools can play a vital role in this.

'There are things that schools can do – including for all their pupils, for those showing early signs of problems and for families exposed to several risk factors – to intervene early and strengthen resilience, before serious mental health problems occur'. (Mental health and behaviour in schools, departmental advice for school staff, DfE 2015)

Teachers and school staff have direct contact with children on a daily basis and may be the first to spot mental health problems. They are also often the first people parents turn to when they are worried about their child. This doesn't mean that teachers and school staff should become mental health specialists, but it does mean that they are well placed to support the positive mental health and emotional well-being of all children, to spot signs of emerging problems, and to provide early interventions – including knowing when to refer on, if necessary. But how confident are we in our ability to notice the early signs of mental health problems in our children?

2. 'Many adults are not confident in being able to spot the signs of poor mental health in children.'

This statement is TRUE and noted by Dr Raphael Kelvin, Child psychiatrist and clinical lead for the MindEd programme. According to a Populus survey in 2014, commissioned to look at adult awareness of children's mental health, many adults report a lack of confidence in their ability to spot signs of childhood mental health difficulties such as depression and anxiety. It seems that when it comes to the issue of our children's mental health, many of us are afraid of getting it wrong and making things worse.

In order to play a central role in early identification, school staff need support and training to be able to develop the necessary confidence, knowledge and skills. Given this, you'd probably think the link between mental health and behaviour would be an integral part of initial teacher training and subsequent professional development, yet this is an area that teachers often feel has been neglected. According to research commissioned by the NASUWT in 2005, 'Teachers often feel unable to discern between mental health problems and emotional/behavioural difficulties'. Consequently mental health problems continue to be misidentified, misunderstood and are often mistaken as 'bad' behaviour. In a press release announcing the *Mental health and behaviour in schools guidance*, the education minister at the time, Elizabeth Truss, was reported as saying:

> 'At the moment too many young people are unfairly labelled as trouble-makers when in fact they have unmet mental health problems.'

For children with mental health problems, traditional behaviour management strategies alone may be less effective. Alongside clear behaviour management, these children may need more personalised approaches to meeting their needs – approaches based on the identification and understanding of the social, emotional and mental health needs that underpin their behaviour.

3. 'Children with learning disabilities are at much greater risk of having mental health problems than children who do not have learning disabilities.'

This statement is TRUE according to research carried out at Lancaster University by Eric Emerson and Chris Hatton. It has been estimated that children with learning disabilities are up to six times more vulnerable to mental health difficulties. There are many factors that can contribute to this, including the fact that children with learning disabilities are statistically more likely to live in disadvantaged circumstances. However, pupils with special educational needs and learning disabilities often face additional challenges in school that can impact negatively on their mental health. These children may have greater difficulty communicating with others, which in turn affects their ability to form friendships and positive relationships. They typically face greater challenges with problem-solving, reasoning and making sense of their world. This can impact on their self-esteem, confidence and their ability to learn and bounce back from difficult situations.

Having special educational needs and learning disabilities is one risk factor for mental health problems, but there are many more. For example, social disadvantage, difficult life events and family breakdown can all increase the risk of mental health problems. It is vital that we understand the range of factors that can place children at greater risk, as well as the signs that indicate a child may be developing mental health problems.

4. 'Half of all lifetime cases of diagnosable mental illness begin by age 14.'

This statement is TRUE and noted by the Royal College of Psychiatrists. Therefore, intervening early to support mental health in childhood makes sense, especially when we know that many forms of mental illness often start in childhood and persist throughout life.

It is estimated that one in four of us will experience a mental health problem, such as anxiety, depression or panic, each year (*Mental health facts and statistics*, www.mind.org. uk). So even if we are not personally affected by mental health difficulties, we are likely to know someone who is. Too many of us will be affected by the impact of mental health difficulties – difficulties which may have been prevented or lessened if they had been identified and supported earlier.

Working towards reversing a lifelong prognosis of mental health difficulties involves a twofold approach:

- promoting positive mental health in childhood
- identifying and supporting emerging problems before they take hold.

Many children will rely on adults in school to initially recognise and support their mental health challenges. This means that school staff need to understand the fluctuating mental health of children and have the confidence to recognise what is typical and what signals concern. It also requires them to understand the factors that place children at greater risk, as well as being alert to the signs of early distress and emerging problems.

5. 'The most important predictor of adult life-satisfaction is emotional health, both in childhood and subsequently.'

This statement is TRUE according to the paper, *What predicts a successful life? A life course model of well-being*, The Economic Journal, 2014. In it, the authors suggest that emotional health and well-being is a far greater predictor of future success and happiness than academic achievement. Therefore, as well as being alert to the signs of mental health difficulties and associated risk factors, it is important to promote awareness of positive mental health, well-being and resilience. But positive mental health doesn't simply mean an absence of mental health difficulties. So, what does it look like?

What does positive mental health in childhood look like?

In order to understand and identify emerging mental health problems, it is helpful to understand and identify good mental health first.

In their publication, *Childhood and Adolescent Mental Health: understanding the lifetime impacts*, the Mental Health Foundation has described children who have good mental health as being able to:

- 'Develop psychologically, emotionally, creatively, intellectually and spiritually.
- Initiate, develop and sustain mutually satisfying personal relationships.
- Use and enjoy solitude.
- Become aware of others and empathise with them.
- Play and learn.
- Develop a sense of right and wrong.
- Resolve (face) problems and setbacks and learn from them.'

A common theme underpinning definitions of positive mental health is the ability to bounce back from adversity. Life will always have its ups and downs and our mental health may change from time to time depending on life events and circumstances. Someone with good mental health won't be permanently positive or happy, but will be better able to cope with what life throws at them and navigate life's bumpy road with no long-term adverse effects.

An important part of positive mental health promotion in school lies in developing staff awareness of the protective factors associated with mental health, as well as the risk factors. For example, our positive mental health and well-being can be influenced by individual characteristics such as gender, personality and age. Some of us may be natural optimists with a 'glass half full' outlook on life, while others may have a natural tendency to gaze into half empty glasses. While we may be limited in what we can do to influence some of these individual factors, there are several environmental factors and experiences that can support positive mental health, making it more likely for children to build a buffer against stressful events and situations. For some children, school may be one of the few places where they will have this opportunity.

Although thinking about the impact of environmental factors and experiences for positive mental health and well-being is important for all children, it will be crucial for some of them.

Whole school approaches, including clear and meaningful behaviour and anti-bullying policies, a culture of sharing concerns that places a high value on positive interpersonal relationships, and well embedded Personal Social Health and Emotional education (PSHE), can support many of these opportunities for all children. In Chapter 2 (page 17), we will address some of the things schools can do to promote positive mental health and resilience. As well as promoting positive mental health and resilience, we also need to understand some of the things that can place children at greater risk of mental health problems. Awareness of the common risk factors, alongside the confidence to recognise the warning signs of emerging problems, is vital for early intervention.

Identifying emerging mental health difficulties: risk factors and early warning signs

Risk factors

Children's mental health can be influenced by a range of different risk factors. Commonly, they can be categorised into the following areas:

- Risk factors in the child
- Risk factors in the family and wider environment
- Risk factors related to significant life events.

Remember! The presence of any of these risk factors doesn't automatically mean a child will go on to develop mental health problems. Some children will have risk factors present in their lives and maintain positive mental health. These children will have protective factors that enable them to be resilient in the face of adversity. However, when there are a number of risk factors and fewer protective factors, this increases the likelihood of a child encountering mental health difficulties.

Risk factors in the child

Individual factors in the child, such as personality, temperament and physical illness can all impact on coping strategies and resilience and affect the likelihood of developing mental health problems. Risk factors in the child also include the presence of learning disabilities, communication difficulties and neurodevelopmental conditions such as autism. While children with these factors can have positive mental health, we know that the impact of living with these risks can increase vulnerability. For example, 'a recent study showed that as many as 71% of children with autism will have mental health problems, such as anxiety disorders, depression and obsessive compulsive disorder (OCD)' (*Tom Madders*).

Many of the descriptors of positive mental health in childhood, such as the ability to get along with others and empathise with them, to play and learn, and to resolve problems and setbacks, can be affected by the presence of additional learning or communication challenges. For example, children with communication needs may have difficulty expressing their thoughts, feelings and wishes, or they may have difficulty understanding what is said to them and making sense of the world. These communication problems can make it difficult for children to get along with others, form friendships and to play positively – all skills that are typically present in children with good mental health. In the same way, cognitive difficulties can affect reasoning and problem-solving skills, increasing the challenges for children to learn though play and to reflect on social situations and generalise new learning to different situations. Children with learning difficulties or disabilities may be less equipped to explain how they feel and to share their concerns, which can add to their distress. When a child has difficulties learning and achieving in school, this can contribute to feelings of isolation, low self-esteem, less engagement with learning, and a sense of not 'belonging'.

Risk factors in the child are highlighted in Chapter 3 of this book (page 27).

Risk factors in the family and wider environment

There are certain events, situations and experiences that occur within families and the wider environment that can place children at increased risk of mental health issues. Some of these factors include:

- Family breakdown
- Parental conflict and domestic violence
- Parental mental health problems
- Parental substance misuse or criminality
- Chaotic, inconsistent or harsh parenting, and rejecting relationships.

Some children come to school burdened with worries and concerns about living in the modern world. They may have picked up on parental anxieties about money or work, or live with violence or abuse. Social and environmental factors that are known to increase risk of mental health problems in children include:

- Living in poverty or economic disadvantage
- Homelessness.

In these circumstances, children's changing emotional needs may not be met at crucial points in their lives, resulting in children who lack security, consistency and a sense of having their emotions understood and managed. In school, the breakdown of friendships and lack of positive friendship groups can also increase risk. Children who lack secure friendships in school may feel more isolated, be more vulnerable to negative peer pressure, discrimination and bullying. If these children also don't have the opportunity to establish a good relationship with an adult in school, then their risk of mental health problems increases.

Risk factors in the family and wider environment are highlighted in Chapter 4 of this book (page 65).

Risk factors linked to significant life events

Significant life changes or traumatic events can also place children at greater risk. Life changes and traumatic events can include:

- Changing schools
- Transition from primary to secondary school
- Moving house
- The birth of siblings
- Bereavement
- Parental separation or divorce
- Exposure to natural disasters and war.

Many of these events involve an element of change and loss, whether that is loss caused through bereavement, abuse, neglect, violence, accident or injury. Some children will face difficult life events and manage to cope, but we know that some children may be at greater risk. For example, we know that looked-after children, who often face multiple losses and trauma, are particularly vulnerable to mental health problems, and that, *'almost half of children in care have a diagnosable mental health disorder'* (DfE 2015).

Risk factors linked to significant events are discussed in Chapter 5 of this book (page 99). Children will respond to the presence of risk factors in different ways, and for many children a short-term change in behaviour may be a typical coping response. In order to effectively support children through difficult situations and circumstances, we need to understand what is a typical coping response for each individual child and remain alert to the early warning signs that indicate a child may need more support.

Early warning signs

It is often easy to recognise when children are physically unwell – they might look visibly different, or tell you they feel in pain or uncomfortable. But mental health isn't always like that. Children often don't understand their feelings, or can't find the words to express their worries or anxieties. It can also be difficult to recognise what is a 'typical' emotional response that all children experience from time to time, and what might signal an emerging mental health problem. In many cases, the first sign of an emerging mental health challenge will be a *change* in behaviour. Any significant change in behaviour should be noted and monitored closely, thinking about things such as:

- The child's age and developmental stage – is this behaviour a typical age appropriate or developmental response?
- The severity, complexity and persistence of the behaviour
- What has and hasn't worked in terms of managing the behaviour
- Whether the change in behaviour could indicate other needs, including unmet learning needs, medical needs or safeguarding concerns
- The presence of any risk factors for mental health problems.

What might early warning signs look like to school staff?

Early warning signs for staff could include:

- **An increase in 'acting out' behaviour such as aggression, disruption, and non-compliance** – How is the child getting along with other children and adults? Are there more conflict situations in school? Think about behaviour in unstructured and structured situations, for example in the playground and in the classroom.
- **An increase in 'acting in' behaviour such as withdrawal, isolation, lethargy and a lack of motivation** – Does the child appear tired or switched off? Are they less noticeable than before?
- **A change in response to learning** – Is the child less able to concentrate or more easily distracted? Do they have trouble remembering, and take longer to problem solve or process information? Are they more likely to opt out of learning, dismiss their work and disengage?
- **An increase in anxiety** – Are they anxious in situations where previously they had no issues? Do they appear increasingly fearful and worried about seemingly minor events? Do they seek reassurance in more and more situations? Are they increasingly alert or hyper-vigilant, on guard or restless?
- **An increased reliance on rituals, or an increase in repetitive behaviour** – Has the child developed new routines and rituals or are they becoming increasingly rigid and dependent on familiar routines and behaviours?
- **A change in physical appearance** – Has their state of dress changed, or their posture, skin tone, hygiene or cleanliness?

Remember! It is a change in behaviour that is often the key indicator of difficulties.

What might early warning signs look like to parents?

Parents know their children best and it is important to listen to their concerns. However, they might not immediately recognise their child's change in behaviour as a sign of an emerging mental health problem. Their initial concerns may be focused on the impact on the family and how to manage the behaviour. Again, it is important to be alert to concerns about a *change* in behaviour. Early warning signs of mental health problems that a parent might alert you to, could include:

- **Sleep difficulties** – including difficulties getting off to sleep, staying asleep throughout the night, or having recurring nightmares.
- **Behaviour at home that is increasingly difficult to manage**.
- **Worries that their child doesn't want to go to school any more, or no longer wants to play with friends**.
- **Changes to their child's personality or appearance** – they might describe their child as more sad, withdrawn, tired or tearful.
- **Reference to physical symptoms in their child that can't be medically explained** – this could include change in appetite, sudden weight gain or weight loss, sickness, complaining of headaches or aching joints.
- **Concerns about self-harm** – such as scratching, cutting, biting, pulling out hair or eyelashes or making themselves sick.

What might early warning signs look like to children?

Children may not always be able to recognise or express their concerns or distress but they might say that they:

- **Feel worried, sad, angry, upset or scared**
- **Feel sensations in their body** such as a racing heart, or feel breathless and shaky
- **Are having trouble concentrating** and can't do their school work anymore
- **Are having troubles with their friends**, feel picked on or bullied
- **Hate themselves**, feel like hurting themselves or don't want to live.

Remember! There can be many underlying factors that contribute to a change in behaviour. It is important to consider emerging mental health issues when thinking about the range of factors.

When emerging mental health difficulties are suspected, staff should monitor the behaviour closely, usually over an agreed time period, and provide early support and intervention. This could include seeking advice and input from other professionals. The case studies in this book provide a framework for identifying risk factors, thinking about whether the child's behaviour could reflect mental health concerns, and planning appropriate early support.

But before we think about identification and early support for mental health problems, let's think about what schools can do to promote positive mental health for all children.

At a glance. . .

Understanding children's mental health

- We all have mental health. It affects how we think, feel and behave. When children have positive mental health they are more likely to get along with others, play and learn, and bounce back from setbacks.

- Three children in every class could have a diagnosable mental health *disorder*, but many more are likely to have mental health *problems*.

- Mental health disorders have a negative impact on academic achievement and all mental health problems, such as worry, stress and anxiety, can interfere with learning.

- Risk factors for mental health problems include:

  ○ Risk factors in the child – such as personality and learning disabilities

  ○ Risk factors in the family and the wider environment – such as family breakdown, parental mental health problems, economic disadvantage and homelessness, or being isolated from peers

  ○ Risk factors linked to significant life events – such as changing schools, the birth of siblings, bereavement, abuse, neglect, accident or injury.

- The presence of risk factors doesn't automatically mean a child will go on to develop mental health problems, but being aware of the risk factors means we can be more alert to potential difficulties.

- A typical sign of mental health difficulties is a *change* in behaviour.

- Parents are likely to talk about changes in their child's behaviour, especially if this is having an impact on life at home. They may not recognise this as an indication of a possible mental health problem.

- Children may not be able to recognise or express their concerns or distress, but they might say things like they feel worried or picked on, that they can't concentrate anymore, or hate themselves.

- When staff suspect a child's behaviour is linked to emerging mental health problems, this should be monitored and early support and intervention provided. This includes referring on to other agencies when necessary.

'Are all adults in your school aware of the risk factors for mental health problems, and can they recognise the early warning signs that might signal emerging mental health difficulties?'

2 Promoting positive mental health and resilience in school

If emotional health in childhood is 'the most important predictor of adult life satisfaction' (see Chapter 1, page 9), then investing in children's mental health makes sense. But what does this mean in practice?

The key to mental health support in schools is twofold:

1. Provide universal approaches to promote positive mental health for all.

2. Provide targeted support for those children experiencing mental health challenges.

In this way, targeted individual support is built on a foundation of whole school commitment to promoting positive mental health, enabling those with emerging problems to be identified and supported early. Even though those children who face several risk factors are likely to benefit most from a focus on positive mental health, whole school approaches will benefit everyone.

Resilience

We know that some children, despite facing risk factors and significant adversity, manage to cope. These children seem to draw on resources that act like a buffer, helping them to handle, and survive, the challenges that they face.

> 'Seemingly against all the odds, some children exposed to significant risk factors develop into competent, confident and caring adults.' (Mental Health and Behaviour in Schools, DfE)

But we also know that some children won't face significant risk factors but nevertheless will struggle to cope with the general ups and downs of daily life. Although these children don't necessarily have mental health problems, it doesn't mean that they have positive mental health either.

So why do some children cope better than others?

When we search for the reasons why some children can navigate their way through challenge and adversity, we often hear the term 'resilience' somewhere in the response. Resilience and mental health are closely linked, and promoting resilience can lead to better mental health. Universal approaches in school that promote awareness of mental health and well-being, and which support development of the inner and external resources children need to be resilient and thrive into adulthood, are arguably as important as the academic curriculum.

What is resilience?

Resilience is a vital part of our positive mental health. The word 'resilience' comes from the Latin *resilire*, meaning to rebound or spring back, and resilience is often described as the ability to 'bounce back' from adversity. This doesn't mean being permanently optimistic, or never experiencing negative or difficult emotions. Even the most resilient children can have mental health challenges, but resilient children are more likely to be able to work though difficult emotions and challenges and continue to thrive afterwards.

Nor is resilience reserved only for severe challenge and adversity. We all benefit from the capacity to be resilient in our daily lives. It is part of life to face challenge in various forms. Everyday events like missing the bus and being late, or misunderstandings with friends or colleagues, can cause feelings of stress and anxiety. It's often through experiencing stressful situations like these, and learning how to manage them, that we develop the skills and resources to survive – and survival doesn't only mean getting through it, but learning, adapting and thriving. Therefore the term 'bounce forward' is sometimes used to reflect the aspect of resilience that involves being able to move on, learn and adapt through adversity and challenge.

> *So is resilience something we are born with, like brown eyes or curly hair? Or is it something that can be acquired or learned given the right conditions? Can we plant the seed of resilience, water it, feed and nurture it until it begins to take hold and grow?*

Although studies suggest that resilience is linked to personality or character traits, this seems to be only a small part of the story. Public Health England's document, *Local action on health inequalities: Building children and young people's resilience in schools*, 2014, discusses how we may be born with a tendency to be resilient, but it is our experiences, opportunities and relationships, that shape and impact how our resilience develops. These factors – including the environment we live in, our families, social supports, and economic circumstances – have been termed the 'social determinants' of resilience, emphasising the fact that our resilience isn't fixed from birth but affected by everything around us.

This document also highlights the link between social support and resilience, as illustrated in a study which looked at how elderly people 'bounced back' after adversity in their lives. Irrespective of personality type, education history or socioeconomic status, the study found that the one thing these resilient elderly people had in common was the presence of someone they could trust and rely on in a crisis. And it was the availability of this social support that enabled them to work through and manage their challenges.

We all need resilience, but it is complicated, and it is not always possible to pinpoint the reasons that enable one person to be resilient, and another less so. Resilience can be multifaceted, fluctuating and influenced by different things. However, protective factors can provide the conditions to enable resilience to thrive. If children can experience these protective factors they can act as a buffer against adversity and help them cope with challenge. So, if resilience is something that can flourish under the right circumstances, how can we enable more children to experience these circumstances?

Promoting resilience in school

Many children will be living with risk factors that schools have limited capacity to change. They may be living in poverty or facing homelessness, their caregivers may be inconsistent or chaotic or suffering from mental health or addiction problems, they may have experienced close family bereavement or they may have been removed from abusive households into the care system. Some children may be living with several of these risk factors.

Although schools may have limited control over many of these risks, they can help to counteract their impact by promoting protective factors within the school environment. For some children this may help to redress the balance between risk and protective factors in their lives. And it can make a difference. . .

Protective factors

Thomas Hébert's study of children living in extremely adverse circumstances looked at the things that helped them to achieve in school, despite adversity. Some of the protective factors were summarised as:

- Having supportive adults and peers around them who want to achieve
- Having access to a range of extra-curricular activities
- Having supportive and challenging educational experiences
- Having a strong self-belief and sense of who they are.

Similarly, in the Young Minds document, *The Resilient Classroom* (Taylor, Hart and Hove Park school), five areas are considered in relation to resilience. These are:

- 'Basics
- Belonging
- Learning
- Coping
- Core self'

As well as noting the importance of relevant learning opportunities and support to develop coping strategies, inner strengths and beliefs, this document also notes the need for 'basic' underpinning structures, such as good housing and diet. Of particular importance is the opportunity for children to establish a sense of 'belonging' in their school environment. A sense of belonging or 'connectedness' in school is a recurrent theme in studies of resilience. In the document, *What works in promoting social and emotional well-being and responding to mental health problems in schools?*, Weare, 2015, 'connectedness' is described as, 'a feeling of being accepted, respected and bonded to the school environment', and an important protective factor for positive mental health.

Many schools will benefit from initial awareness raising of protective factors for children's mental health before planning how to promote and prioritise these factors within the school ethos and environment. The Young Minds resilience handout is cited in the Dfe document, *Mental health and behaviour in schools* and both documents can provide further reading on the factors that can help promote resilience and positive mental health.

In the case studies, some of the relevant protective factors for positive mental health and resilience are highlighted.

What key experiences, opportunities and skills support children's positive mental health, well-being and resilience in school?

Studies suggest that resilient children benefit from:

A secure base with a range of supports in order to develop a sense of belonging and security. In school this not only means a safe and predictable physical environment, but also opportunities to experience safe and supportive relationships with adults and other children. From this secure support base, children are then able to acquire:

The internal skills and beliefs that enable them to develop a sense of self-worth and competency. In school this includes experiencing achievement and supportive challenge, safe in the knowledge that they may not always be immediately successful. One important internal belief is self-efficacy – the sense that personal actions can make a difference, and an understanding that working towards challenges and goals may involve effort and setbacks. Children develop a sense of self-efficacy through being heard and supported to work through problems, but also through observing and learning from the social experiences and the problem-solving of others.

Opportunities to experience, observe and practise a range of social, interpersonal and problem-solving skills. An ability to problem solve and manage interpersonal relationships is a protective factor for future adversity and challenge. In school this includes investing in, and delivering, a curriculum that values relationships, emotional understanding, communication and social problem-solving.

These three building blocks of resilience are reflected in the work of Edith Grotberg who studied the opportunities, experiences and skills that children need in order to maintain positive mental health and be resilient. In *'A guide to promoting resilience in children'*, 1998. She highlighted three sources of resilience that children need to draw from, as follows:

1. I HAVE

- People around me I trust and who love me, no matter what
- People who set limits for me so I know when to stop before there is danger or trouble
- People who show me how to do things right by the way they do things
- People who want me to learn to do things on my own
- People who help me when I am sick, in danger or need to learn

2. I AM

- A person people can like and love
- Glad to do nice things for others and show my concern
- Respectful of myself and others
- Willing to be responsible for what I do
- Sure things will be all right

3. I CAN

- Talk to others about things that frighten me or bother me
- Find ways to solve problems that I face
- Control myself when I feel like doing something not right or dangerous
- Figure out when it is a good time to talk to someone or to take action
- Find someone to help me when I need it

These three sources (I have, I am, I can) interact together and children need to draw on all of them in order to develop resilience.

So what could these three sources of resilience look like in school?

The three sources of resilience in school

1. I HAVE

For some children, school might be one of the few places where they can experience the external supports necessary to build the foundations of the 'I have' source of resilience.

These external supports include having supportive, nurturing, predictable and consistent environments, as well as people who can provide relationships that are also supportive, nurturing, predictable and consistent. Children need these external supports to form a solid foundation upon which to build their inner strengths and skills. As we heard in the previous study with resilient elderly people, these external supports will continue to be important throughout life, and are vital building blocks for resilience and positive mental health.

In a resilience-building school a child would say:

- **I have adults in school who focus on the positive mental health and well-being of everyone, and who know how to identify and support those with emerging problems**. In a resilience-building school, staff will prioritise an understanding of child development so that they know what is a normal part of growing up and what signals cause for concern. They understand the link between mental health, behaviour and achievement and this understanding underpins the school ethos and approach. This includes awareness of the needs of their own well-being as well as the children's!

- **I have adults in school who understand my local community and the stressors and risk factors facing our families**. All members of staff are committed to working closely with parents to fully understand the impact of community and family stressors, before working in partnership to plan support when it is needed.

- **I have adults in school who teach me how to behave by showing me, and focus on helping me to understand and manage my feelings**. Members of staff in an emotionally resilient school seek to understand the message behind the behaviour first. Behaviour support systems and pastoral support work together to share strategies and approaches with a focus on helping children. Behaviour support is underpinned by a relational framework that helps children to: understand and manage emotions, establish positive relationships and develop social problem-solving skills. They work with all of the adults in the child's life, including the family, to explore how best to support behaviour, and use real-life situations as opportunities to help children reflect and problem-solve so they are better equipped to manage future situations.

- **I have adults in school who are able to identify my individual learning needs and provide personalised support when I need it so I can do my very best to become an independent learner**. While staff in emotionally resilient schools will support positive mental health for all children, they will have processes in place to identify those individuals who are most at risk and who will benefit from a personalised approach and targeted support. They will have good understanding of the risk and protective factors for positive mental health and early indicators of mental health problems. For example, they will understand the importance of having at least one strong adult relationship as a protective factor and, while promoting positive relationships for all children, they will be aware of the need to implement key adult support for those who are most at risk, especially around times of transition and change.

- **I have adults in school who have good links with local agencies and support services, so they can access other forms of support when I need it.** Resilient schools don't work in isolation, they are part of a community hub and work to establish and maintain links with a variety of agencies to meet children's needs.

When children have access to these resources in school they are provided with a secure and predictable base from which they can go on to build their inner sources of resilience.

2. I AM

Grotberg describes the 'I am' factors of resilience as 'the child's internal, personal strengths. These are feelings, attitudes and beliefs within the child.' These self-beliefs are an important part of positive mental health and resilience and are closely linked to self-efficacy – the belief that one's own actions can make a difference. The 'I am' source of resilience can therefore instil a sense of hopefulness and possibility in children that is vital for the capacity to bounce back from adversity. While some of these characteristics may arguably be dependent on things like temperament and personality, there are things we can do in school to help children shift their reliance from the external 'I have' to encompass the internal 'I am' sources.

In a resilience-building school a child would say:

- **I am liked and valued and I belong**. Children know that adults care about them and that they will be treated with fairness and consistency. Consequently, children have confidence in school and feel that they belong.

- **I am encouraged to care about the needs of others around me, even when they are different to my own**. Children are helped to understand the needs of others and their beliefs through whole school approaches as well as direct teaching about diversity, strengths, differences and tolerance. Children are encouraged to celebrate their own achievements as well as the achievements of others.

- **I am able to make the most of my personal strengths, both curricular and extra-curricular, and am supported in any challenges I might face**. Positive achievements help to build resilience. Therefore a resilience-building school creates many opportunities for children to celebrate positive achievements, not only academically but also in extra-curricular areas as well. Members of staff demonstrate by example that achievements and success sometimes involve perseverance, effort and determination, and staff link praise and reward to effort as well as success.

- **I am able to make a difference because my views are heard and considered**. An important part of mental health and well-being is believing that what you say or do matters. In a resilience-building school, children have many opportunities to have a 'voice' and to be heard. This may be through school councils, student user groups or pupil profiles, but also in the way staff model relationships which value and respect others. When children have the internal belief that they can make a difference, this helps them to develop the skills they need to be involved in meaningful activities, work through difficult situations and persevere to achieve their goals.

3. I CAN

When children have supportive environments and people around them to build resilient inner beliefs and attitudes, they are then able to develop the interpersonal, communication and problem-solving skills that will enable them to work though difficult and challenging situations. Grotberg describes this as the 'I can' source of resilience. Children need this source of resilience in order to get along with others, solve problems and handle a range of emotions, including negative thoughts and feelings. In school this means having opportunities to develop and practise these skills safely.

In a resilience-building school a child would say:

- **I can talk about my thoughts and feelings**. Resilient schools offer a language of emotions, as talking about feelings and how to manage them is the norm. Although a focus on well-being and mental health permeates throughout a resilience-building school, there are also curriculum opportunities to target teaching about mental health and well-being based on the needs of the children. Children's behaviour is seen as an opportunity to notice and name emotions and to explore ways of managing emotions in a socially acceptable way.

- **I can practise problem-solving in a safe environment, explore how to negotiate solutions and find ways to move forward**. Children are encouraged to see different points of view when problem-solving, and to take these into account. Staff help them to find a range of ways forward, test out solutions before they act, and introduce creativity and humour whenever possible.

- **I can manage my behaviour in a safe way**. Children are taught that while all emotions are acceptable, the consequent behaviour may not be, and they are helped to find ways of self-calming and managing their behaviour in a way that is acceptable to others. Members of staff model their own emotional and behavioural regulation and support children to find strategies that work for them.

- **I can understand my behaviour and that of others, and how behaviour is linked to thoughts and feelings**. Children are helped to make links between their thoughts, feelings and behaviour so that they understand how their thinking impacts on what they do. Members of staff help children to understand that other people's behaviour can also be affected by their mood and temperament and help them to take this into account when interacting with others.

- **I can find someone in school who I can trust to help me**. Children know that they have trusting relationships with adults around them who will be there to support them when it is needed. Staff also know the importance of positive peer support and find ways of establishing supportive peer relationships, such as buddies, mentors and peer supporters.

Positive mental health and resilience is important, and we can all benefit from learning how to keep ourselves mentally healthy so we can cope with life's challenges – whatever they may be. The earlier we learn to be mental health aware, the more likely we are to adopt mentally healthy lifestyles and habits. It is similar to physical fitness. David Stalker, CEO of UK active says, 'We know that generally active children become active adults,' and when positive habits and patterns for physical exercise are laid down in childhood, they are more likely to sustain a commitment to physical exercise into adulthood. The same can be applied to our mental health: positive mental health habits established in childhood can set out a blueprint for how we look after our mental health and well-being throughout our lives.

Although some determinants of resilience may be within the child and linked to personal traits, research suggests that the social determinants of resilience play a big part in developing a positive sense of well-being. This incudes the environment we live in, the relationships with the people around us and the experiences and opportunities we have available to us. For some children, school may be one of the few places where they can experience the sources of support that are needed to develop the inner beliefs, attitudes and skills that enable them to have hope, persistence and resilience.

It's a fact of life that things won't always go to plan. One of the most important lessons we can teach our children is how to acquire and maintain the skills needed to cope with challenge and adversity.

At a glance. . .

Promoting positive mental health and resilience in school

- Universal approaches to promoting positive mental health for all children need to underpin targeted support for those children experiencing mental health challenges.
- Resilience is a vital part of our positive mental health. Resilient children are more likely to be able to work though difficult emotions and challenges and continue to thrive afterwards.

- We all benefit from the capacity to be resilient in our daily lives. Resilience not only means coping with challenge, but also learning, adapting and thriving.

- Our experiences, opportunities and relationships all shape and impact on how our resilience develops. These determinants of resilience emphasise the fact that our resilience isn't fixed from birth, but is affected by everything around us.

- To develop resilience, children need a secure base with a range of social supports in order to develop positive internal skills and beliefs and social, interpersonal and problem-solving skills.

- Edith Grotberg notes that children need to draw resilience from three sources:
  - 'I have' – the things that are available to me in my environment.
  - 'I am' – the characteristics and traits that make me who I am.
  - 'I can' – the things I can do (or learn to do) with the support of others.

- For some children, school may be one of the few places when they can experience these sources of resilience.

 'How do staff in your school work together to promote children's resilience?'

3 Risk factors in the child

Although risk factors rarely occur in isolation, the sections in this chapter particularly focus on the impact of risk factors in the child. Risk factors in the child can include things such as:

- learning difficulties
- communication difficulties
- neurodevelopmental difficulties (such as autism spectrum disorder (ASD), attention deficit hyperactivity disorder (ADHD), dyspraxia and dyslexia)
- physical illness
- individual personality and traits
- genetic influences.

The following sections focus on how risk factors in the child can impact on mental health and behaviour, highlighting some of the risks associated with speech, language and communication needs, autism spectrum disorder (ASD), and inattention and impulsivity problems. However, the 'Five step framework' encourages us to be curious about all the risk factors that may be present.

Using the case studies

The purpose of the case studies is to highlight some of the risk factors that can impact on mental health and behaviour. However, it is important to remember that the presence of risk factors does not necessarily lead to mental health problems, but that awareness of risk factors and warning signs can help inform early identification and support. As such, the case studies are not intended to be used as a diagnostic tool, but to provide examples of using a five step framework when considering behavioural concerns.

The children in the case studies don't exist but reflect some of the typical concerns shared in consultations. Please note that the consultation questions were worked through over a series of sessions.

Speech, language and communication needs (SLCN)

Case study: Adam, Year 3

Consultation process overview

Following the five step framework

STEP 1. **What can we see?** The first step is to summarise the concerns about Adam's progress, starting with a description of his behaviour, and thinking about how often it occurs, how long it lasts and where it usually happens.

STEP 2. **What have we tried?** Reflecting on the strategies and interventions already tried in school, and their impact.

STEP 3. **What do we know?** Bringing together what we already know about Adam. In order to consider a wider perspective, this includes incorporating Adam's own views and the views of those who know him best, such as his family, as well as looking at information held in school.

STEP 4. **What is the mental health message?** Reflecting on what we understand about Adam's difficulties, thinking about risk factors and warning signs, to consider a link between mental health and behaviour. Can we identify or predict any emerging mental health problems?

STEP 5. **What would personalised planning look like for Adam?** Finally, in light of this understanding how can we best support him? How can we strengthen protective factors for mental health and implement targeted mental health support?

Step 1: What can we see?

ℚ What his teachers say...

Adam isn't making any progress. He seems to have come to a total standstill academically which, of course, is a major concern for us. Now he regularly refuses to engage in classroom activities and requests, especially those that involve writing. At first he started putting his head on the desk and refusing to pick up his pencil, but his behaviour has become even more challenging. He now runs out of the classroom when he doesn't want to participate. Only last week he ran out of the classroom on three separate occasions in one day. When we talk to him calmly and clearly to remind him of the rules and encourage him to make good choices, he becomes distressed very quickly. He cries and shouts and becomes quite hysterical. It can take a long time to calm him and encourage him to re-engage in the classroom.

His general behaviour is steadily worsening but, apart from a refusal to write, there aren't always any obvious triggers. He becomes angry very quickly, almost as if a switch is flicked inside him. When he becomes distressed he often swears, shouts and cries. This takes up a lot of adult time and energy and is also extremely disruptive for the rest of his class. On occasion, he has lashed out when he is upset. This doesn't appear to be intentional, but more as a result of his distress and frustration, but nevertheless we can't condone his behaviour and we are worried that if it continues he might physically harm someone, or be excluded.

The other children seem to like him, especially when interacting with him on a one-to-one basis. He is very good at sports and everyone wants him on their team. But I can see that they are becoming more wary of him now because his behaviour can be so extreme and they don't know how he might react. It's usually in the playground and when working in groups in the classroom that problems occur. Adam falls out with others very easily. He finds it hard to juggle relationships and interactions in groups with other children. It can be really difficult to leave him in a small group where he has to share equipment or ideas. It always ends in conflict, with Adam storming off in a huff or a temper. This often happens when he can't get his own way. He is quick to blame other children, and never accepts his own role in conflicts. He describes everything as someone else's fault.

We haven't had any major concerns about his learning, although we did wonder about the possibility of dyslexia, so he works in one of the groups that receive an extra boost for literacy. He is more confident and able in numeracy and science. We do feel that Adam is choosing to only participate in those lessons he enjoys or feels come easier to him.

Step 2: What have we tried?

ℚ What his teachers say. . .

We are following our whole school behaviour management strategies to try to support him. For example, Adam receives sanctions for his inappropriate behaviour and we use a traffic light warning system to remind him about his behaviour and to encourage him to make 'good choices': good behaviour is green; amber then red for when he is beginning to make poor or inappropriate choices. This doesn't seem to be having much effect, partly because so much of his behaviour is unpredictable.

We have a support plan in place following the school's behaviour policy where we have set out the consequences of his aggressive behaviour. We have reward charts in place, but Adam seems to lose interest in them very quickly and they don't really seem to motivate him.

We also make sure his work is differentiated to meet his needs so he is able to have some success and achieve. He receives an extra boost for literacy in small groups. The problem is he now won't make any attempt when he thinks work is too difficult for him, even though we don't ask him to do work which is beyond his ability.

We have carried out literacy assessments and involved one of the teachers who has dyslexia training. These assessments suggested he is 'at risk' of dyslexia with particular difficulties around *phonological skills (his ability to manipulate sounds in spoken words) and working memory. We have made a referral to the advisory support teacher to look into this further.*

Step 3: What do we know?

📄 Summary of key information from Adam's school file

- A speech and language report was written two years ago when Adam was in Year 1. The referral was made because of concerns about his spoken (expressive) language skills. The initial speech and language therapy assessment resulted in a six-week block of therapy. Adam attended a few sessions but was eventually discharged for non-attendance. The discharge speech and language report noted that his spoken language skills appeared a little improved and that he was more confident when talking to others. He continued to have some word finding difficulties. This meant that Adam sometimes chose the wrong word or needed extra time to think of the word he wanted to use in some situations.

- The speech and language therapist reported that his receptive (understanding) language was still an area of concern. He needed extra time to process verbal information, make sense of what was said to him, and to think of his response. The speech and language therapist thought he struggled to process complex longer sentences, and often didn't understand key words or vocabulary. She made some recommendations and suggested a further referral if there were any future concerns.

- Adam hasn't received any further speech and language input and his current teacher wasn't aware of the previous concerns about his understanding of language.

- Adam has achieved within the lower end of the age expected range during Key Stage 1 with the exception of literacy where he is working below the expected levels.

🔍 What his parents say. . .

Adam can be a lovely boy at home, when he wants to be. He is happiest when he is playing on his bike or his computer. He is also a very good footballer and plays for the local team on a Saturday. As he gets older, he is having more and more anger management problems. I know his teachers have noticed this as well. He gets especially angry with Lucy, his little sister. He seems to take his anger out on her, which is very difficult to manage.

Homework has always been an issue with Adam, but recently it has become even more difficult to get him to do it. I dread the whole homework thing. I know that even if we are having a good day, as soon as I mention the 'h' word he will just blow. To be honest, sometimes I don't even try any more. It's not worth the bother as I can't deal with the fallout.

Since he's gone into Year 3 Adam says he hates school, calls himself 'thick', says no one likes him and that he doesn't want to go to school anymore. Some mornings I can hardly get him out of bed. Mondays are a nightmare. He takes no notice of me anymore and I can get so frustrated with him. When I ask him to do something for me, such as go upstairs and fetch something from the bedroom, he often just wanders off and does his own thing. He is taking less and less notice of me and I feel like I am always nagging him. It's not good for anyone.

Adam is popular with the other children in his class, he gets invited to parties but doesn't seem to have any close friends. He falls out with his friends when playing in the street – if there's any trouble you can guarantee Adam will be in the middle of it. He tells me the others pick on him and I think there could be some truth in this. I think the others know he gets easily wound up, and kids will be kids, they know which buttons to push.

○ What Adam says. . .

Adam didn't want to talk about his problems in school but was happier drawing things he likes and things he finds 'tricky'. Adam shared his views with the teaching assistant who he knows very well. He did this by drawing pictures and comic strips about his likes and dislikes, what he finds difficult in school and what helps him. This can help Adam develop some self-awareness so that he is actively involved in deciding how others can best help him, as well as how he can help himself. This information was then written into a personal profile, which Adam agreed could be shared with his teachers and others in school.

Adam's Personal Profile

Things that are important to me

- I like to draw. I especially like drawing animals. My teacher says I am a good artist.
- I like to ride on my bike with my friends. I have a silver mountain bike that I clean with the hosepipe when I have been for a ride.
- I like to play football at the weekend. I never miss a training session.
- I like to have friends at my house. I like to have lots of friends.
- I like playing computer games with my friends but I don't like it so much when I don't win.
- I like PE and art best of all in school.

Things I find difficult

- It upsets me when my friends are unfair or pick on me.
- I don't like writing. I find it hard to remember how to spell words and my wrist hurts when I have to write.

- I find literacy tricky. I like stories but not when I have to read them myself.
- I find it hard to remember everything I need for school in the morning.
- Sometimes it is hard to remember what I have to do in class, and I always lose my pencil and pen.
- It's hard keeping my temper when I get in trouble for leaving my seat.

Things you need to know about me

- I prefer to draw rather than write. It sometimes helps me to remember things better if you draw pictures as you talk to me.
- I don't always understand why my friends fall out with me.
- I don't know why people get mad at me.
- It helps if you spend some time going over what has happened using drawings and pictures.

Step 4: What is the mental health message?

Given what we now know about Adam can we identify any emerging mental health challenges, or an increased vulnerability of developing mental health problems? What are the risk factors and warning signs?

Key points from the consultations

- Adam's behaviour has recently changed.
- He is non-compliant in school and often argues with his friends.
- At home he is described as having 'anger management' problems.
- His behaviour is worse when working in a small group and in unstructured situations, such as in the playground. It also deteriorates in the classroom when he is asked to write.
- At home, he refuses to do his homework and forgets instructions. His mother feels he ignores her.
- He is 'at risk' of dyslexia and receives extra literacy support.
- He has a history of speech and language difficulties.
- He can usually make his needs known in general conversation, but he sometimes chooses the wrong word or needs extra time to think of the word he wants to use.
- His understanding of language is of greater concern. He may need extra time to process verbal information, make sense of what is said to him, and to think of his

response. He may struggle to process complex longer sentences and may not understand key words or vocabulary.

- Adam says he has trouble remembering things and doesn't like reading or writing.
- He likes drawing best of all.
- He doesn't understand why his friends fall out with him.
- Behaviour management strategies have had little effect.

Could his behaviour reflect any emerging mental health problems?

Emerging mental health problems – risk factors and warning signs

1. Change in behaviour

Adam's change in behaviour could be a sign of emerging mental health problems. Adam's behaviour has been monitored and behaviour management strategies implemented, however, the usual behaviour management strategies aren't working and his behaviour seems to be worsening. These concerns are shared by school staff and by his mother. Although his behaviour can be unpredictable, his difficulties are particularly apparent when interacting in groups with other children and also when he is asked to write. School staff have addressed some of his literacy challenges by giving him extra support. Despite this, his behaviour continues to deteriorate.

It is possible that Adam's behaviour is linked to difficulties understanding and communicating with others, as well as linked to literacy difficulties. Speech, language and communication difficulties are not always easy to identify and can often be mistaken as something else, such as behavioural issues. Some children with unsupported speech and language difficulties may also develop mental health problems due to the impact of social isolation and frustration. Adam may need a more personalised approach to meeting his individual needs, including approaches to support possible emerging mental health challenges.

2. Speech, language and communication needs

Adam's speech, language and communication problems are a risk factor for mental health issues. Adam has a history of speech and language problems, especially understanding what is said to him. Adam's behaviour difficulties are often linked to social relationships and difficulties interacting with others. It may be more challenging for him in group situations to understand and to process information fast enough to keep up with the conversation. We know that young people with speech, language and communication difficulties can have poor conversational skills, poor non-verbal skills and poor social understanding. All of these things can hinder their ability to form friendships and may increase feelings of isolation, leading to emotional problems such as anxiety and low mood.

3. Learning challenges

Adam's learning challenges could make him more vulnerable to mental health issues. Adam dislikes literacy and has a negative perception of himself as a learner – he describes himself as 'thick'. He opts out of writing tasks and his behaviour can become challenging when required to engage in literacy activities. He no longer completes his homework and doesn't want to go to school. Many children with speech, language and communication needs have associated difficulties acquiring literacy skills, and Adam's reluctance to engage in tasks could indicate specific difficulties in this area, as well as a lack of understanding and confidence in himself as a learner. Adam may not be able to ask for support or express how he is feeling, and his aggressive outbursts could be linked to these frustrations.

Conclusion

We recognise that Adam's behaviour could reflect mental health challenges – there are several risk factors that increase his vulnerability, and there are some signs to suggest that mental health challenges could underpin his current behaviour. Therefore, staff should consider personalised approaches to support Adam that take these factors into account.

Step 5: What would personalised planning look like for Adam?

A personalised approach would need to consider whole school approaches and systems to support Adam, including:

- Adam's ongoing assessment needs and how staff will monitor and measure his mental health challenges and know when to refer on
- Building In review schedules in order to continue to share information with school staff and the family about his progress and ongoing needs
- How the pastoral support system can support Adam, for example, considering the need for a key person and or counselling support
- The need to refer Adam to other services for support and advice, for example, speech and language therapy and advisory teacher or educational psychology support for his learning needs.

Protective factors for good mental health and resilience

As well as supporting mental health challenges, a personalised approach would build on protective factors for good mental health and resilience (See Chapter 2, page 17). Some of the protective factors for good mental health include:

- Being able to communicate needs and desires, and being able to establish positive interactions with others.

- Having the opportunity to experience success and a sense of achievement.

- Creating a positive school climate where Adam can feel that he is valued and belongs.

- Being supported to understand his personal strengths as well as support to work through and solve problems.

Therefore, a personalised approach for Adam would include strategies to support his speech, language and communication needs, as well as thinking about how to prevent further social isolation, stress and anxiety and how to help him develop a more positive perception of himself as a learner.

Some specific strategies and approaches to support Adam's individual needs include:

1. Supporting his expressive (speaking) and receptive (understanding) language needs

This could be achieved by:

- Giving him extra time to listen to, and understand what is being said

- Speaking in short sentences, with pauses and at a slower pace – it might also help to emphasise key words

- Asking him to summarise back, in his own words, what has been said to ensure he fully understands

- Using information Adam has shared about what helps him best – this includes drawing pictures or symbols when talking to him to help him remember and understand what has been said

- Introducing him to important new vocabulary before it is needed in the classroom

- Giving him lots of opportunities to speak to different people in different situations in school to develop his expressive and receptive language

- Cueing him in carefully to discussions in the classroom, always using his name first to attract his attention, asking him questions directly and giving him time to think of his response.

2. Supporting his behaviour by developing his social and interaction skills, and social understanding

This could be achieved by:

- Helping him to understand social situations and his role in them – encourage him to draw what happened, step-by-step, when reflecting on challenging social situations as this will help his verbal expression and understanding and also provide a visual reminder that he can refer back to. Support Adam to sketch out who was there, what they did, what they said and what they may have been thinking. In this way Adam can be supported to link his own actions, thoughts and feelings, as well gain insight into the actions, thoughts and feelings of others. (See 'Comic strip conversations' below.)

- Helping him to practise communicating positively during play and interactions – use role play to help him rehearse what to say and do in social situations, how to disagree with others in an acceptable way, and how to tell others when he is upset, worried, confused or frustrated.

Comic strip conversations
(Carol Gray)

'Comic strip conversations [are] designed to illustrate and simplify conversations with simple drawings.' (Carol Gray).

The Comic strip conversation approach can help to 'clarify communication' with 'an emphasis placed on what people may be thinking.' In this approach children are encouraged to draw step-by-step what happened, what was said and what people may have been thinking, as a visual way of reflecting on social situations. Colour can be used to 'identify the emotional content of statements, thoughts and actions.' In this way children can be helped to understand the complexity of social interactions and conversations, and to explore a range of solutions to future situations.

For a more detailed explanation of comic strip conversations see Carol Gray's book, *Comic Strip Conversations*.

---

3. Supporting his emotional awareness and emotional regulation, and helping him to recognise and express his frustration and anger in ways that are socially acceptable

This could be achieved by:

- Linking emotions to how his body feels and encouraging him to use strategies such as using a 'calm card' to show he knows he needs some time out. For example, 'I can see you are breathing heavily now, I wonder if you are getting frustrated about something. Let's get the calm card and take some time out'.

- Assigning a key person to talk through incidents with him using pictures and drawings as suggested opposite, and then helping him to explore ways of managing his strong emotions by making a list or resource box of 'self-calming' activities.

- Keeping an 'emotions and triggers diary' (see page 95), noticing the events and situations that are his personal triggers, naming the emotions that are triggered, and recording what helps him to notice and manage his emotions.

- Creating a classroom atmosphere where it is ok to ask for help. Adam's behaviour is sometimes linked to his literacy difficulties. He may be reluctant to ask for help and draw attention to his difficulties. Classroom strategies such as turning over a card on the desk to signal the need for support may be more acceptable.

4. Supporting his learning challenges and promoting a positive perception of himself as a learner

This could be achieved by:

- Raising awareness of his strengths and incorporating his interests to develop his self-esteem. In Adam's case, this includes his love of art, physical activities such as football and P.E, and working on the computer.

- Differentiating tasks and simplifying written material in clear and understandable vocabulary.

- Linking praise and reward to effort rather than success. This will help him to understand that he can persist when faced with challenge.

- Creating a classroom environment where it is accepted that everyone will make mistakes because that is how we all learn. Model making mistakes yourself and explain your learning from them.

- Ensuring homework is differentiated and accessible. Think of other ways he can record information, e.g. voice recording, mind maps, pictures and drawing.

- Seeking support from professionals to understand further how best to support his learning challenges.

At a glance. . .

Speech, language and communication needs (SLCN)

- Speech, language and communication difficulties are a risk factor for mental health problems. Children with communication difficulties may have problems making themselves understood as well as understanding others. This can affect their ability to make lasting and positive friendships leading to feelings of isolation, frustration, anxiety and stress. All of these factors can impact on their mental health. If these difficulties remain unidentified, related mental health problems can become worse as a child grows older.

- Speech, language and communication difficulties are not always easy to identify and can often be mistaken as something else. When children are unable to express themselves, or understand what is said to them, they can develop behavioural issues because of their frustration. Therefore speech, language and communication difficulties may be mistaken as behavioural difficulties.

- Many children with speech and language difficulties will have difficulties with literacy skills. While having speech language and communication problems does not necessarily mean an individual will have learning difficulties, there is a strong link between speech, language and communication needs and literacy problems.

- When supporting children with speech, language and communication needs, remember to:

  - Think about supporting any related mental health issues as well as speech and language skills, e.g. think about how to prevent social isolation, how to reduce stress, anxiety and frustration, and how promote confidence and self-esteem.

  - Consider the need for targeted pastoral support, such as assigning a key person or individual counselling.

  - Consider using visual strategies, such as comic strips and drawing. These strategies often help children to process and understand the complexities of social interactions, as well as developing greater social understanding and emotional awareness.

  - Think about supporting children to recognise and express their feelings in sociably acceptable ways. This could include reflecting on situations using drawings and pictures, noticing and naming emotions for them, and practising positive ways to manage feelings together.

  - Create lots of situations for the child to interact positively with others around school. This could include offering small group work to develop and practise social skills.

  - Consider the need to support any literacy difficulties or other learning challenges.

- Incorporate the child's interests and strengths to develop self-esteem and confidence. This could include developing a personal profile with the child to help all staff understand the child's individual needs and views.

- Think about involving other professionals to help clarify the child's needs.
- Build in regular reviews with staff, the child and the family to share information about progress and any further needs.

 'Can you think of any children whose behaviour may be linked to unidentified speech, language and communication problems?

Autism spectrum disorder (ASD)

Case study: Jodie, Year 5

Consultation process overview

Following the five step framework

STEP 1.   **What can we see?** The first step is to summarise the concerns about Jodie's progress, starting with a description of her behaviour, and thinking about how often it occurs, how long it lasts and where it usually happens.

STEP 2.   **What have we tried?** Reflecting on the strategies and interventions already tried in school, and their impact.

STEP 3.   **What do we know?** Bringing together what we already know about Jodie. In order to consider a wider perspective, this includes incorporating Jodie's own views and the views of those who know her best, such as her family, as well as looking at information held in school.

STEP 4.   **What is the mental health message?** Reflecting on what we understand about Jodie's difficulties, thinking about risk factors and warning signs, to consider a link between mental health and behaviour. Can we identify or predict any emerging mental health problems?

STEP 5.   **What would personalised planning look like for Jodie?** Finally, in light of this understanding, how can we best support her? How can we strengthen protective factors for mental health and implement targeted mental health support?

Step 1: What can we see?

✑ What her teachers say. . .

As a school, we are finding the whole situation with Jodie quite frustrating. She has a diagnosis of autism spectrum disorder (ASD), which she received in Year 4. To be honest, we were quite surprised about this, as in school she doesn't really present with many issues at all.

We got the impression that her parents thought that something different would happen in school as a result of the diagnosis. For instance, that Jodie would receive extra support or provision. We explained that she was making good progress in school and didn't need anything different from the other children in her class.

However, since starting in Year 5 we have had several phone calls and meetings with Jodie's parents about her behaviour at home. They describe her as bad tempered, defiant and unmanageable. They say Jodie is very angry when she gets home from school in the evening, often shutting herself in her bedroom and refusing to engage with the family. When they encourage her to leave her room and join the rest of the family, her behaviour gets worse. They describe her as 'flipping out'. When this happens they say she targets her elder sister and lashes out at her. They tell us that this is having a big impact on their family life.

It is really difficult for us in school, as we don't see any of this behaviour. In school, Jodie is a quiet, amenable member of the class. She is making good academic progress and is one of the most able students. She doesn't stand out at all. She particularly enjoys reading and would stay in the library all day if we let her. She enjoys fairy tales and we see her re-enacting some of the stories with the younger children in the playground.

Although she is not the most sociable of girls, she doesn't isolate herself from the others. If you see her in the playground she probably wouldn't immediately stand out. She is not a loner and doesn't wander around by herself or play in her own world isolated from the other children. At break times she often enjoys sitting on the bench making friendship bracelets next to a group of girls. You can see her laughing and trying to join in. She does seem to prefer to be with the younger children in Year 3. We think this is because Jodie enjoys being in charge and she can direct the younger children more easily than the girls her own age.

On occasion, there have been a couple of incidents in class when she has fallen out with the other children – girls in particular – and some girls have described her as 'bossy'. She has one particular friend in her class and when she is absent or not present in the classroom Jodie does miss her and often asks for reassurance about when she is coming back. We think she over relies on this girl. However that said, many of the other children in class have similar ups and downs with friendships too, and none of these issues seem particularly out of the ordinary.

We are at a bit of a loss about where to go next as her parents are increasingly demanding and insistent that her behaviour at home is because of her diagnosis and management in school.

Step 2: What have we tried?

⌕ What her teachers say. . .

Jodie is progressing very well academically, therefore we haven't needed to provide any in class support for her learning. She works very well independently but sometimes has more difficulty working in groups with other children. She can't always tolerate their mistakes and she can sometimes get a little frustrated with them. She also gets upset when others don't agree with her, or want to do something in a different way. When this happens she doesn't act out or behave inappropriately, but tends to do her own thing, working alongside rather than with, the others.

Sometimes other children complain about her 'bossiness' – or need to get her own way. When this happens we spend some time talking through what has happened to try to help her understand that others might not always learn as quickly as she does, or might have another viewpoint. We manage the group work carefully by putting her in a smaller group with more tolerant children. However, apart from the usual classroom strategies and support to talk through disputes and friendship worries, Jodie doesn't really need any extra support.

Because of parental concerns we started a home-school diary, but we usually struggle to write anything in it other than, Jodie 'has worked well', or 'had a good day', but this seems to upset her parents even more. They write reams about her behaviour at home – it's as if we are looking at two different children. Her parents say that Jodie is unhappy at break time and lunchtimes and are worried that she is left alone. Even though we have reassured them that Jodie is not isolated and usually plays with other children, they have asked us to provide her with a buddy. We have resisted this so far as we don't think there is a need. We don't want to make an issue of her autism if we don't have to.

Step 3: What do we know?

📄 Summary of key information from Jodie's school file

- A multi-agency report from the previous year notes that Jodie received a diagnosis of autism spectrum disorder. The paediatrician had seen Jodie at her parents' request a number of times from the age of six because of their concerns about her development. Jodie didn't immediately receive a diagnosis of autism as she didn't appear to meet all of the criteria, such as displaying high enough levels of restricted interests and repetitive behaviour. However, there were significant concerns about her understanding in social situations and how she communicated and interacted with others, so she was kept under review. She received a diagnosis of autism when she was eight years old.

- The paediatrician says that, at first glance, Jodie's interests and routines can appear quite typical for a girl of her age, for instance she is very interested in soap operas and boy bands. However, over time it has become apparent that it is the quality of, and her reliance on, these interests that are different. Jodie can become quite obsessed with her interests to the point that they rule her life at home. For example, Jodie will go to her room after school and listen to the same CD over and over again with no interest in listening to new songs from the same group, widening her experience by listening to similar groups to see if she likes them too, or choosing to share her interest with others in a social way. She will watch soap operas avidly and can recite chunks of the storylines word for word. If she misses one of her soaps, or if she has to do something else after school that prevents her from listening to her songs, she can became very upset and distressed.

- The speech and language therapist reported that Jodie has very good speech and a wide and mature vocabulary for her age. This can sometimes mask her social communication difficulties. Jodie finds it very difficult to understand the nature of social interactions and how to behave and respond. She prefers to talk about things that interest her, or to respond to direct and clear questions. She particularly struggles with social chit-chat and establishing friendships with others. As Jodie is very intelligent she will try to copy the actions of others around her in an attempt to fit in. For example, she might laugh at a joke along with the other children, but this does not mean she understands why they are laughing, or that she 'gets' the joke.

- There are no concerns about Jodie's academic achievements or progress, and she is achieving within or above age expected levels in all areas.

◌ What her parents say. . .

We are so worried about Jodie, it's difficult to know where to start. Even though she has just recently got the diagnosis, her behaviour at home has had a massive impact on the family for years. We always knew there was something different about Jodie's development, and we are glad that we can now put a name to it in the hope that it will help us all.

To sum it up, Jodie's autism affects every aspect of our family life and it has become steadily worse over the past few months. We are ruled by what Jodie does and doesn't want to do. For example, she never wants to go out at weekends or on an evening anymore, and as we can't leave her alone, we are totally led by her. If we try to insist that we do something different, even just go to the shopping centre, she will totally flip out – so we no longer suggest it.

It sounds as if we have totally spoiled her, and sometimes it feels that way, but we think that it is all just too much for Jodie and she needs to hide herself away and do the things she likes to do, just to switch off. The problem is that this behaviour is getting worse. Now she doesn't just refuse to leave the house. . . she also refuses to leave her bedroom! She is becoming more and more withdrawn and isolated. She won't even join us to watch her soaps any more – something she used to do regularly. Now she insists on watching them alone in her room. When we have tried to get her to come and join us, she has become violent – lashing out at me and her sister – or become so distressed that she has made herself physically sick. She says she hates being her and that no one understands her. What can we do? It's true.

We know she is very different at school and, while we are glad she knows how to behave there, we also find it very frustrating. How can she be so different for us at home? It makes us wonder if we are doing something very wrong. We feel as if the teachers don't always believe what we say. Who can blame them – they've never seen this side of her.

We are so worried that there will come a point where she will refuse to leave her room at all. She has started to say she feels sick on a Monday morning and doesn't want to go to school. We have taken her to see the doctor, but he can't find any medical reason for her nausea, and asked if perhaps she is being bullied in school. We followed this up with her teacher who assured us that this isn't the case and that Jodie is happy in school and has some friends. We're just not sure though, because Jodie gets so upset and insists that she doesn't want to go to school anymore. She has had a few tantrums about this, but so far we have always managed to get her there. By the middle of the week she seems to be back in the routine and it's usually not so bad. But it starts all over again every Monday morning and gets worse after a holiday or half-term. We are dreading the summer break. We don't know how she is going to manage settling back in to Year 6, and we don't want to think about moving on to secondary school!

We know everyone thinks we are fussing but we don't know what to do.

$\bigcirc$ What Jodie says. . .

Jodie was keen to talk about her interests and hobbies, but in order to encourage her to think more widely about her likes, dislikes and challenges, staff used prompt sheets and questionnaires to help keep Jodie focused. The information was used to produce a pupil profile for Jodie. This can be used during transition planning to help her new teacher understand her better, and to help Jodie think about her own strengths and challenges.

Jodie's Personal Profile

Things that are important to me

- I like to watch all of the soaps on TV. My favourite is Coronation Street, but I like them all. I like to remember the stories and what the characters say so I can pretend to be them.

- My favourite group is One Direction and I like to listen to their songs. I like to close my bedroom door and not be disturbed when I listen to them. It makes me feel better.

- I like to read books and I like my favourite fairy tales. I like to read them sometimes at school and sometimes at home. At playtime I like to do plays about the fairy tales. I like to give out the parts and tell my friends what to say and do. I like being a director and might want to make films or soaps when I grow up.

Things I find difficult

- Sometimes I get annoyed when my friends don't listen to me. I get especially annoyed when they don't listen to me when they are wrong and I am right. When this happens, it helps me to pretend they don't exist.

- I don't like it when my mum wants me to go downstairs when I am tired. Sometimes I want to be left alone. After school I feel very tired and sick and being in my room makes me feel better.
- I don't like some of the noises that other people make when they are working, like when they click their teeth – I hate that; it makes me feel sick.
- I don't like it when my sister bugs me to do things I don't want to do.

Things you need to know about me

- Sometimes I want to be by myself to rest and do my favourite things.
- I don't always understand things that happen in the playground, especially when people fall out and become cross and angry. It's the same when we do group work. There's always fuss and bother.
- If you want me to do something, it helps if you explain why you want me to do it, for how long and when it will end.
- I don't like going places where I know there will be lots of people, especially people I don't know. This makes my head hurt and then I feel sick.

Step 4: What is the mental health message?

Given what we now know about Jodie, can we identify any emerging mental health challenges, or be alert to an increased risk of developing future mental health problems? What are the risk factors and warning signs?

Key points from the consultations

- Jodie has a diagnosis of autism spectrum disorder. This affects her understanding of social situations and her ability to interact with others.
- She has some age appropriate interests and hobbies but she can be very intense and obsessive about them.
- She is doing well academically.
- Her behaviour is good in school – she doesn't appear isolated but she prefers to play with younger children and finds it more difficult to interact in groups of children her own age.
- She tries to interact with others, including in groups, but often finds this confusing.
- Jodie has one special friend but can over rely on her and struggles when this friend is not available.

- At home her behaviour is worsening. She is isolating herself more and more in her room, and says she doesn't want to go to school.

- Her parents report that she is particularly irritable at the end of the school day, hides herself away in her room and becomes aggressive if disturbed.

- She often complains of feeling physically unwell – headaches and sickness.

Could her behaviour reflect any emerging mental health problems?

Emerging mental health problems – risk factors and warning signs

1. Diagnosis of autism spectrum disorder

Jodie's diagnosis places her at increased risk of mental health problems. Jodie has a diagnosis of autism, and while we know that children with autism can have good mental health we also know that having autism can make people more vulnerable to mental health problems. For example, we know that:

'71% of children with autism will have at least one co-occurring mental health problem,'

and

'The most commonly reported mental health problems that the children [with autism] had experienced were anxiety (85%), behavioural issues including defiance and non-compliance (62%) [and] depression (36%).' (Tom Madders)

But it's not always easy to identify mental health problems in children with autism. Children with autism have difficulty understanding and expressing emotions, and this can add to difficulties detecting early signs of mental health problems. It can also be difficult to unpick what is a sign of a mental health problem such as anxiety, and what is part and parcel of autism. Generally speaking, any change in mood or behaviour should alert us to potential mental health difficulties. This could include an increase in obsessional behaviour, refusal to leave the home, threats of self-harm, or increased aggression. So, for instance, if a child with autism becomes even more reliant on routines and rituals we might need to question if this is related to increased anxiety and stress. Noticing subtle changes in the child's reasons for engaging in repetitive activities can be important. For instance, does the child appear more compelled to engage in repetitive activities, rather than wanting to do this for pleasure and enjoyment? Jodie is increasingly relying on her favourite activities and interests when she returns home from school. Her parents explain this as a change in her behaviour as Jodie appears more compelled to remain in her room and isolate herself from the family, and increasingly obsessive about her interests to such an extent that it is having a much greater impact on family life.

2. Change in behaviour

Jodie's change in behaviour could be a sign of mental health challenges. Although Jodie's behaviour hasn't changed during the school day, her behaviour is worsening at home, especially on her return from school. It is not uncommon for children with autism to be able to appear to manage during the school day, but for their stress and anxiety to tip over once they get home after school. Some children with autism explain that they feel heightened levels of stress and anxiety because of the number of interactions they have to manage throughout the school day. Things like keeping up with the conversations around them, trying to understand jokes, work out sarcasm and read non-verbal signals, as well as figuring out the complexities of friendship groups, can all be incredibly stressful. All of these demands can take their toll, so that by the end of the day they feel totally worn out.

For many children with autism, their inner anxiety isn't immediately obvious through their own facial expressions or body language, and they may be working hard to try to copy their peers and try to 'fit in'. So, on the surface, they may seem to be coping well. Sometimes it's only when children get home at the end of the day – tired, confused, and physically and emotionally wrung out by trying to survive in the social world – that their real stress levels become apparent. Sometimes these children increasingly withdraw into their own obsessions and interests in an effort to relax and self-regulate. At other times their stress might manifest itself as frustration, aggression, and low tolerance for family members around them.

3. Unexplained physical symptoms

Jodie's emotional difficulties present as physical symptoms which can't be medically explained. Jodie often says she feels sick when she finds something difficult or challenging and is increasingly isolating herself from the family. She says she doesn't understand why her friends do and say the things they do, and she doesn't like being in groups. Sometimes girls with autism can appear quite socially able and comfortable at first glance. Indeed, Jodie doesn't appear isolated in school and interacts in social groups with only minimal difficulties. However, Jodie may be working extremely hard to keep up this pretence and hide her difficulties in order to fit in. Jodie repeatedly says that situations make her feel 'sick' even though these symptoms have no medical cause. Many children express their emotional distress by complaining of headaches, stomach aches or feeling generally unwell. When these physical symptoms aren't caused by a medical problem, they can often be a sign of mental distress.

Conclusion

We recognise that Jodie's behaviour could reflect mental health challenges and there are several risk factors that increase her vulnerability. Jodie is at increased risk of mental health problems because of the impact of her autism. Although her difficulties are more visible at home, she is voicing her reluctance to attend school and we can predict that if her apparent stress and anxiety continue, this will begin to impact on her ability to access the curriculum and continue to make progress. Therefore staff should consider personalised approaches to support Jodie that take these factors into account.

Step 5: What would personalised planning look like for Jodie?

Whole school approaches and systems

A personalised approach would consider whole school approaches and systems to support Jodie, including:

- How the pastoral support system can support Jodie, for example, thinking about the need to access counselling or individual support to help her identify, communicate and manage her thoughts and feelings.

- Providing a key worker for Jodie to help her develop a positive relationship with an adult in school, and who can check in with Jodie at agreed points during the day to preempt any further difficulties.

- How to monitor and review her progress, including knowing when to refer on for more specialist support if necessary.

- The ongoing professional development needs of staff to support understanding of autism, including how autism can present in boys and girls, and how children with autism can experience some mental health challenges.

- Transition planning for her new Year 6 class, as well as thinking ahead about timely planning for her transition to secondary school – this could include the involvement of support services such as local advisory support teams for autism, and educational psychology support.

- Supporting Jodie's parents to understand and manage behaviour at home, exploring links with parenting support groups to share other families' experiences of managing autistic behaviour.

Protective factors for good mental health and resilience

As well as supporting mental health challenges, a personalised approach would promote protective factors for good mental health and resilience. (See Chapter 2, page 17) Protective factors for good mental health include:

- Creating a positive school climate where Jodie can feel a sense of belonging and connectedness, with good relationships between home and school
- Having the opportunity to participate in a range of activities and experiencing achievement and success
- Developing Jodie's range of problem-solving approaches
- Promoting her social and communication skills
- Creating an environment that promotes the identification and sharing of worries – where school and parents communicate openly, support each other and work together.

A personalised approach for Jodie would consider ways to support her social understanding and social comfort, to help her develop positive relationships and feel a sense of belonging, and to help her to recognise and manage her stress and anxiety in a socially acceptable way.

Some specific strategies and approaches to support Jodie's individual needs include:

1. Supporting Jodie to identify her own and others' emotions

This could be achieved by:

- Using a range of photographs to identify and name emotions in other people, and to reflect on times when Jodie feels similar emotions. Keep these photographs in a scrapbook for Jodie to refer to from time to time.
- Using Jodie's interest in role play to act out social situations to help her understand what others may be thinking and feeling and why they do the things they do.
- Helping her to think about different social situations in school and how they can elicit a range of thoughts and feelings. Children with autism are likely to find it challenging to reflect on abstract situations, to understand things from another person's point of view, and to recognise the range of emotions that people may experience. Using visual strategies, such as drawing while talking can help communication about thoughts and feelings. Strategies such as Carol Gray's 'Comic strip conversations' (see Chapter 3, page 36), 'Social Stories™' and using mind maps can all be useful. Try to make the abstract more explicit through visual strategies.

Carol Gray

'The goal of a social story is to share accurate information meaningfully and safely.' (Carol Gray)

Social stories were developed by Carol Gray and can be a useful tool to help people with autism and learning difficulties to understand specific events or challenging situations, and to develop social skills. Social stories usually consist of simple sentences written in the first person to describe situations or events. These sentences describe what might happen and what others might do, and share perspectives of what people might think or feel. Directive sentences are also used to indicate what the individual can try to do when in the target situation. Therefore social stories can often lead to improved social understanding, which in turn can lead to improved behaviour.

For guidelines on how to develop social stories see Carol Gray, *The New Social Story™ Book*

2. Supporting Jodie to express and manage her emotions

This could be achieved by:

- Using visual aids such as rating scales (with numbers from one to ten) or thermometer gauges to help describe the intensity of an emotion and to recognise when Jodie needs to use strategies to regulate and manage her emotions.

- Helping Jodie to identify her personal triggers for stress and anxiety. This could include sensory triggers, e.g. Jodie has mentioned she finds teeth clicking irritating. Carry out a sensory profile with Jodie to gain greater understanding of her sensory issues and to reduce her potential stress. Work with Jodie and her family to think about the different places in and around school that could cause her sensory distress. She could also keep a diary to help her link when she feels stressed and anxious to trigger situations.

- Helping Jodie explore a range of things she can do when she recognises her emotions are intensifying. This could include practising what works for her and using some of her special interests to help her self-regulate. These could be written down as a series of prompts to remind her of what she can do in times of stress. For example, 'when my anxiety gets to a 5, I can go and listen to my music for five minutes to calm down before returning to the group'. Jodie could practise a range of different strategies with adult support.

- Teaching Jodie to let others know when she needs to take some time to manage her emotions or when she needs support. For example, she could have a red card which she turns over on her desk as a sign for the adults in the room.

3. Supporting her social communication and interaction skills

This could be achieved by:

- Using 'Social Stories™' as described above and situational scripts to explain how others behave in social situations and what Jodie can try to do.
- Helping Jodie participate in small structured group activities to teach and model positive social skills.
- Using role play and 'comic strip conversations' (see page 36), to reflect on what has happened and to consider what she might do differently next time.
- Encouraging her to interact with others in different situations, for example taking part in extracurricular activities that she might find interesting, such as a drama club.

4. Helping Jodie to think of and practise acceptable ways to self-regulate and relax

This could be achieved by:

- Negotiating how she might be able to use her special interests to help her relax and recharge her batteries. This might include going to her room after school to listen to music for a set amount of time. Encourage her to recognise when she feels more relaxed.
- Working with her parents so Jodie knows everyone is aware of the agreed strategies. Build on strategies used in school that can also be used at home. When Jodie is comfortable using her relaxation strategies, work with her to explore other strategies to expand her range, reduce rigidity and encourage flexibility.
- With her parents' agreement, it may help Jodie to explore her autism diagnosis in a supportive way, thinking about what this means for her and how she can best manage her challenges.

At a glance...

Autism spectrum disorder
- Autism can increase the risk of mental health problems. We know that children can have autism and have good mental health, but autism can increase vulnerability for developing mental health problems.

- The most common mental health problems for children with autism are anxiety and depression. It has been estimated that '71% of children with autism will have at least one co-occurring mental health problem'.

- It's not always easy to identify mental health problems in children with autism. Children with autism have difficulty understanding and expressing emotions, and this can add to difficulties detecting early signs of mental health problems. It can also be difficult to unpick what is a sign of a mental health problem such as anxiety, and what is part and parcel of having an autism diagnosis. Generally speaking, any change in mood or behaviour should alert us to potential mental health difficulties.

- Sometimes a change in behaviour or mood may be most obvious at home. It's not unusual for children with autism to appear to be coping in school but for their stresses and anxieties to spill out at home time. Sometimes these children increasingly withdraw into their own obsessions and interests in an effort to relax and self-regulate. At other times, their stress might manifest itself as frustration, aggression, and low tolerance for family members around them.

- Be alert to sensory sensitivities that can add to anxiety and distress. Carry out a sensory profile with the child and family to think about situations in and around school that might contribute to sensory distress.

- Support for children with autism and mental health problems should include:
  - promoting social understanding and social comfort
  - developing social communication and interaction skills and how to identify, express and manage emotions support to practise self-regulation and relaxation.

- Children with autism can have particular difficulty reflecting on abstract situations that are not in the here and now.
  - Use visual strategies to help keep communication concrete, to reduce anxiety and to promote understanding of social situations and others' viewpoints.
  - Use personal diaries to help children identify individual triggers for stress and anxiety and to explore ways of managing and self-regulating.
  - Use the child's personal interests and strengths to create a feeling of belonging in school, promote confidence and self-esteem, and to interact with others in a positive way.

'Do staff in your school understand how stress and anxiety can manifest in children with autism?'

Inattention and impulsivity

Case study: Nikhil, Year 2

Consultation process overview

Following the five step framework

STEP 1. **What can we see?** The first step is to summarise the concerns about Nikhil's progress, starting with a description of his behaviour, and thinking about how often it occurs, how long it lasts and where it usually happens.

STEP 2. **What have we tried?** Reflecting on the strategies and interventions already tried in school, and their impact.

STEP 3. **What do we know?** Bringing together what we already know about Nikhil. In order to consider a wider perspective, this includes incorporating Nikhil's own views and the views of those who know him best, such as his family, as well as looking at information held in school.

STEP 4. **What is the mental health message?** Reflecting on what we understand about Nikhil's difficulties, thinking about risk factors and warning signs, to consider a link between mental health and behaviour. Can we identify or predict any emerging mental health problems?

STEP 5. **What would personalised planning look like for Nikhil?** Finally, in light of this understanding how can we best support him? How can we strengthen protective factors for mental health and implement targeted mental health support?

Step 1: What can we see?

ℚ What his teachers say. . .

Nikhil is a lovely young boy. He is such a character and he can be hugely entertaining, but his behaviour is becoming increasingly worrying. If I had to sum him up in one word, I would say 'distracted'. Most of the time he seems a million miles away. In class, it is obvious he's not listening, especially during whole class or group time. Sometimes he will be physically distracted by what is happening around him, and he will fiddle with objects and reach out and touch things – including the other children! At other times, he can be physically still and apparently calm, but nevertheless not be taking anything in. He can be extremely impulsive and react immediately with very little thought. For example, although he is getting better at remembering to put up his hand when he wants to speak, he will still blurt out random information. Last week he put up his hand to answer a question in the science lesson and asked me if I dyed my hair!

When it comes to getting on with tasks and completing his work, he has huge problems. He will either wander around the classroom asking other children for help and disturbing them, or sit at his own table staring into space. I don't think he is intentionally disruptive, but the other children will either laugh at something inappropriate he has said, or become annoyed by his constant wandering. I can't say we have any major behavioural outbursts with Nikhil, it is more a case of a constant low-level disruption which has an impact on the class – the wandering around, calling out, lack of focus and generally being off task.

Sometimes Nikhil can sit quietly when he working at his table, but nevertheless he often seems to be in a daydream. At other times he struggles to stay in his seat, looks confused, has difficulty focusing his attention on his work, and struggles to follow instructions. Even when you talk to him directly he doesn't seem to be listening. It's as if he is thinking about other things that he finds so much more interesting. He is making very little progress academically, which is frustrating because when he puts his mind to it he can have some very good and creative ideas. His written work, however, is careless and disorganised.

Recently Nikhil has developed a tendency to twitch and blink repeatedly for a few seconds. He doesn't really seem aware of this, but the other children have noticed and have laughed at him or told him to stop it. We are not sure why he is doing this and there don't seem to be any triggers. On some days these twitches appear worse then others, but there can also be days when we don't see them at all.

He can often be quite clumsy around school. Sometimes he can't seem to walk past a table without knocking something, or someone, over. We don't know if this is because he has a real problem with his balance or coordination, or that he simply isn't concentrating on what he is doing.

Nikhil has always stood out as being immature and much more physically restless and impulsive than the other children. However, now he is in Year 2 his distraction stands out as being much more of a problem. His lack of focus and concentration seem to be getting worse and we are increasingly worried. He is no longer making progress because he simply doesn't complete most of his work.

Step 2: What have we tried?

$\bigcirc$ What his teachers say. . .

We have tried rewarding Nikhil in class when he stays on task and completes his work. Although he loves things like stickers and reward charts, and can be motivated by them for short periods of time, they don't seem to help him to learn and change his behaviour in the long term. We have also tried sanctions for off task behaviour, and have used a report card in lessons to encourage him to concentrate.

In terms of completing his work, we wondered whether it was a case of 'can't' or 'won't' do it. We did consider the possibility of learning difficulties, however, when someone sits with him and physically keeps him on task he is more than capable of doing the work and has some very good ideas. So, when we can, we give him one-to-one support. Obviously this is a huge drain on resources and not something we can offer every day.

We do try to break his work into smaller chunks to make sure we aren't overloading him, and have tried using things like a sand timer to encourage him to stay focused for short periods of time. Unfortunately, the sand timer proved to be even more of a distraction for him than a help!

Occasionally, when his behaviour becomes too disruptive for the class, we ask him to 'do some jobs' for the teacher in the Foundation Stage. We find this gives him, and the rest of his class, some respite. His lack of attention and concentration is not as apparent in a less-structured environment, and he can be helpful and kind with the younger children.

We have talked to his dad about taking him to the GP to get his attention difficulties checked out. However, his dad said he doesn't want him 'labelled'. He says they don't have any problems with him at home. We have also checked out things like his hearing and vision with the school nurse just to make sure they weren't contributing to his difficulties.

Step 3: What do we know?

📖 Summary of key information from Nikhil's school file

- There are no concerns about Nikhil's speech and language skills or general learning and problem-solving skills. Previous assessment in Foundation Stage and in Year 1 indicated that his ability falls broadly within the age expected range.

- His attention and concentration skills have been a concern since he started school.

- He is generally fit and healthy and there are no concerns about his vision or hearing.

- The behaviour intervention team became involved in Year 1 and they carried out some observations and suggested further investigation into his attention difficulties and impulsivity. Suggested strategies included breaking tasks into smaller chunks and using visual prompts to keep him on task, such as using a sand timer. Following this intervention it was suggested that parents take Nikhil to the GP to check out his attention difficulties but this has not yet happened.

💬 What his parents say. . .

I think Nik is just like me. I can get a bit frustrated with all of the complaints about him, because my teachers said exactly the same things about me when I was at school. He's just being a boy – he likes to do boy things: be outside, move about and not sit still listening to others. His mum thinks a lot of his behaviour is because Nik isn't as grown up as the other kids in his class. Perhaps we've spoilt him a bit. He is the youngest of our four children and the only boy. He's also a summer birthday, so he is very young for his age. He's not a mature seven-year-old. When I look at some of the others in his class, girls especially, I think he looks so much younger. So I put a lot of his behaviour down to his immaturity and I think he will grow out of it in time just like I did. His dad and me feel very strongly that we don't want him labelled or medicated.

Nik loves to be outside, read his comics, watch TV and play on his iPad. Sometimes he can be really focused and concentrates well when he is doing something that he likes. I know he can be a bit forgetful and sometimes seems as if he is on another planet... but not all of the time.

Nik had no problems when he was a baby. He fed well, grew well, and everyone seemed happy with how he was doing until he started school. In nursery it wasn't so bad – I suppose he was happy to wander around and do his own thing. Now he's in Year 2 he can't do that anymore and that's why we have a problem.

We have noticed some of his twitching at home. It gets worse when he is tired. He has problems getting himself to sleep at bedtime, so we often let him play on the iPad or laptop in bed until he feels sleepy. We are starting to worry that he is falling more and more behind at school even though he is a bright boy. Its just that he's not getting the most out of school at the moment.

What Nikhil says...

Nikhil drew pictures of the things he likes best and things he finds most difficult. In this way he was encouraged to think about what helps him most in school. With his agreement, this information was then summarised in his individual profile to share with others.

Nikhil's Personal Profile

Things that are important to me

- Playing outside with my friends
- Going fast on my scooter
- Reading my comics – I want to be a comic artist when I am older
- Playing on my iPad.

Things I find difficult

- Doing turns and jumps on my scooter
- Being good in school – I am always in trouble
- Sitting still without fidgeting
- Remembering stuff.

Things you need to know about me

- I am very good at drawing
- I am a fast runner
- I am very fast on my scooter.

Step 4: What is the mental health message?

Given what we now know about Nikhil, can we identify any emerging mental health challenges, or an increased vulnerability of developing mental health problems? What are the risk factors and warning signs?

Key points from the consultations

- There have been longstanding concerns about his attention and concentration problems. These difficulties were first noticed in Reception class and are not improving with age.
- His attention and concentration problems are now having an impact on his progress in school.
- There are no concerns about speech and language difficulties or learning difficulties, however he is not meeting his learning potential in school.
- Sometimes Nikhil can be physically restless, fidgety and impulsive, but most of the concerns are about directing his attention and maintaining concentration.
- Nikhil's behaviour has changed recently and he has developed twitches and repetitive blinking.
- The other children have noticed and commented on his behaviour.
- He can appear clumsy and uncoordinated.
- His parents describe Nikhil as being like his dad. They also attribute some of his difficulties to immaturity. They don't want to involve the GP as they don't want him 'labelled'. However they are worried he is falling behind at school.
- Nikhil enjoys drawing and reading comics and playing on his scooter.
- He dislikes being 'in trouble' at school, and expresses worries about remembering information and feeling confused.

Could his behaviour reflect any emerging mental health problems?

Emerging mental health problems – risk factors and warning signs

1. Problems with attention, concentration and impulsivity

Nikhil's attention and concentration difficulties have been apparent for some time and are impacting on his ability to make progress in school. Nikhil's teachers know that it is common for young children to be inattentive and easily distracted and they have monitored his behaviour since starting school. Now that he is in Year 2, his inattention and distractibility no longer appear age appropriate and are having a significant impact on his ability to learn and make progress. Attention problems and impulsive behaviour can have several underlying causes, including speech and language challenges, learning difficulties, or the impact of adverse early experiences. They can also indicate attention deficit hyperactivity disorder (ADHD). Nikhil does not appear to have any speech and language or learning difficulties, and it is important that school staff continue to talk regularly with his parents to share information about his progress and well-being in school, and explore the pros and cons of referral for further investigations. It will be important to monitor the impact of his difficulties on his mental health and to consider if referral to specialists could support better understanding of his individual needs.

2. Change in behaviour

Nikhil's behaviour has recently changed and he has developed some repetitive twitches and rapid blinking. Nikhil's twitches should be monitored closely to understand more about their frequency and duration, when they typically happen, and to see if they have an effect on Nikhil's functioning. Sometimes stress, anxiety and tiredness can make twitches and tics worse. It will be important to work with his family and to monitor carefully to see whether Nikhil feels under additional anxiety and stress. It is possible that this behaviour could be related to the onset of a tic disorder or Tourette syndrome. Tic disorders can be common in children with ADHD.

3. Impact on self-image

Nikhil's difficulties directing his attention are affecting his progress in school as he is often unable to complete his work. This in turn may impact on his self-esteem and positive self-image as a learner. The school is offering individual support to help him focus and complete work. We know that experiencing success and achievement is an important factor for positive mental health and that academic failure can be a risk factor. Staff and parents have noted that he is underachieving. Nikhil has shared that he dislikes getting 'into trouble' and often feels a sense of 'confusion'. This should be explored further as he may have developed a negative perception of himself in school.

4. Impact on social interactions and friendships.

Nikhil's difficulties could be impacting on his friendships and social interactions in school. Nikhil's peers are noticing and commenting on his behaviour. Having positive peer relationships and a feeing of belonging is important for good mental health. It is important that Nikhil does not feel under pressure from the other children or discriminated against or isolated because of his difficulties.

Conclusion

We recognise that Nikhil's behaviour could reflect mental health challenges and there are several risk factors that increase his vulnerability. These include: demonstrating long-standing attention, concentration and impulsivity problems, a change in his behaviour and the onset of facial twitches, lack of academic progress and achievement, and some indications that his peers are tolerating him less. Staff should, therefore, consider personalised approaches to support Nikhil that take these factors into account.

Step 5: What would personalised planning look like for Nikhil?

Whole school approaches and systems

A personalised approach would need to consider whole school approaches and systems to support Nikhil, including:

- Nikhil's ongoing assessment needs, including planning how to monitor his behaviour and knowing when to refer on if necessary.

- How the pastoral support system can support Nikhil, including the need for key person and/or counselling support to explore ways of promoting his resilience, self-esteem, and problem-solving, and to ensure that he is not feeling isolated or targeted in school.

- Working with his parents to explore referring Nikhil to other specialist services for support and advice, with an emphasis on developing greater understanding of his attention and concentration difficulties and how he can be supported to achieve his potential.

- How staff can work positively with his parents to share an understanding of his strengths and challenges and monitor his progress.

Protective factors for good mental health and resilience

As well as supporting mental health challenges, a personalised approach would also promote protective factors for good mental health and resilience. (See Chapter 2, page 17) Protective factors for good mental health include:

- Having the opportunity to participate in a range of activities and experiencing achievement and success in school

- Having a sense of belonging and positive peer relationships and friendships

- Creating an environment that promotes the identification and sharing of worries – where school and parents communicate openly, support each other and work together
- Receiving support for any learning challenges.

Therefore, a personalised approach for Nikhil would include strategies to support awareness and management of his inattention and distractibility, as well as thinking about how to prevent further social isolation, stress and anxiety and how to help him develop a more positive self-image.

Some specific strategies and approaches to support Nikhil's individual needs include:

1. Supporting his attention, concentration and on task behaviour in the classroom

This could be achieved by:

- Considering the classroom environment and layout to minimise distractions and disruptions. For example, work with Nikhil to think about what will help him best. This could include thinking about his seating arrangements – does he work best at tables with several other children or sitting alongside just one other child? Does he concentrate best sitting near the teacher at the front of the classroom, or at the back where he can see everyone else? Is it best for him to be seated away from the windows, away from the door, etc.?
- Considering how information is presented and delivered to him. For example, think about language use: are instructions given one at a time and repeated? Does it help for him to repeat back in his own words what he has to do? Are verbal instructions supported visually? Can you use colour to outline and organise information that he needs to use? Are tasks presented in segments with clear targets for completing each segment?
- Considering ways to help Nikhil develop his organisational skills. For example, does it help him to use a pointer or bookmark to keep his place on the page and to stay focused for longer? Would it help Nikhil to make notes about what he needs to do in each lesson? Can he use organisers, diaries or visual timetables?
- Legitimising his need for movement by building this into the school day. For example, think about building in tasks for Nikhil such as, 'After you have completed the first activity Nikhil, can you take this package to the Reception class?'

2. Supporting Nikhil's awareness of his behaviour and self-regulation

This could be achieved by:

- Becoming familiar with the early signs of restlessness and inattention. For example, helping Nikhil to better understand and recognise his behaviour may help to reduce or prevent feelings of anxiety and helplessness. Encourage Nikhil's self-awareness by naming his behaviour and supporting him to redirect his attention. This could involve diverting him to a range of less intrusive activities that help him to re-focus and self-calm, e.g. doodling, colouring in, squeezing playdoh. . .

- Working with Nikhil to identify his motivators and offering tokens for on task behaviour to work towards his chosen reward – whole class strategies could be used to encourage children to support each other's positive behaviour and to create a sense of belonging and working towards a shared goal. Strategies such as placing marbles in a jar for positive behaviour (see below) could encourage the class to work towards a shared reward when the jar is full.

- Assigning a key person to talk through incidents with him using pictures and drawings. For example, you could keep an 'emotions and triggers diary', (see page 95) noticing the events and situations that are his personal triggers, the kind of emotions that are triggered, and what helps him to notice and manage his emotions.

- Providing Nikhil with some unobtrusive personal signals to remind him to return to task and to think about his behaviour. For example, this could include turning over a coloured card on his desk, or giving a pre-agreed hand signal. Decide which behaviours can be ignored and which ones will need immediate acknowledgment.

Marbles in the jar

The 'marbles in the jar' strategy can be used as a whole class approach to reinforce positive behaviour and to encourage children to work together and support each other. Be clear about the behaviours you want to encourage. Think about encouraging social behaviours and friendship skills, and display target behaviours on a poster as a visual reminder.

Start with an empty jar and when you notice children displaying target behaviours, invite them to place a marble in the jar. When the jar is full the whole class receives a pre-agreed reward. Talk to the class beforehand to negotiate their whole class reward. This could be an extra five minutes at break time, hearing a favourite story or extra choosing time.

Encourage the class to notice when individuals are displaying target behaviours and to think about how they can support each other to receive marbles. You can vary the size of the jar depending on how long you want the children to wait before receiving a reward. Try to keep the focus on receiving marbles for positive behaviour rather than removing marbles for inappropriate behaviour.

3. Facilitating opportunities for positive social interactions

This could be achieved by:

- Providing opportunities for Nikhil to work with positive role models.
- Providing social skills group work to help Nikhil develop positive relationships, as well as appropriate social skills.
- Supporting his classmates' understanding of diversity and difference through PSHE activities highlighting individual strengths and learning differences.

4. Supporting his learning challenges and promoting a positive perception of himself as a learner

This could be achieved by:

- Raising awareness of his strengths and incorporating his interests to develop his self-esteem. In Nikhil's case this includes his love of drawing, cartoons, and physical activities such as playing on his scooter, working on the computer and IPad.
- Linking praise and reward to on task behaviour and effort, rather than success – this will help him to understand that he can achieve and persist when faced with challenge.

At a glance...

Problems with inattention and impulsivity
- Attention problems, impulsive and hyperactive behaviour can have several underlying causes including speech and language challenges, learning

difficulties, or the impact of adverse early experiences. They can also indicate attention deficit hyperactivity disorder (ADHD).

- ADHD is a condition that includes difficulties with inattention and/or impulsivity and hyperactivity. Only a mental health professional can diagnose ADHD, but it is important to be aware of children who display concentration and attention difficulties and restless behaviour so we can provide early interventions.

- Inattentive, impulsive and hyperactive behaviour problems can have a significant impact on progress and achievement in school, behaviour and social skills. Consequently, these children are at increased risk of mental health problems.

- Other difficulties that can be commonly associated with inattentive and impulsive behaviour include, conduct problems and aggression, learning difficulties, anxiety problems, mood swings and motor tics.

- Support for children with inattentive, impulsive and hyperactive behaviour should focus on strategies to support awareness and management of inattention and distractibility, as well as thinking about how to prevent social isolation, stress and anxiety and how to promote a positive self-image. Think about:

  ◦ The classroom layout and the presentation of tasks, and how these can be organised to minimise distraction and disruption.

  ◦ Remember to think about visual strategies and language use. Does it help the child to repeat back in his own words what he has to do? Are verbal instructions supported visually? Can you use colour to outline and organise information that he needs to use? Are tasks presented in segments with clear targets for completing each segment? Would it help the child to make notes about what is needed in each lesson? Can the child use organisers, diaries or visual timetables?

  ◦ Supporting the child to develop self-awareness of behaviour and to recognise the early signs of restlessness and inattention. This can help reduce anxiety and feelings of helplessness. Assign a key person to talk through incidents, keep an 'emotions and triggers' diary, and model activities to help the child re-focus and self-calm.

  ◦ Promoting positive social interactions and friendships by providing opportunities to work with positive role models, and teaching positive social and friendship skills.

- Using the PSHE curriculum to support other children's understanding of different learning challenges.

- Promoting a positive self-image by using the child's interests and strengths, and linking praise and reward to effort.

 'What classroom strategies do you have in place to support children who present as inattentive and impulsive, and what strategies do you want to develop?'

4 Risk factors in the family and wider environment

Risk factors in the family and wider environment often have a significant impact on how the family functions, including the level and quality of care-giving available to the child and the support which is needed for their development and learning. These risks are often cumulative and can include things such as:

- parental conflict
- family breakdown
- inconsistent or hostile parenting and rejecting relationships
- parental mental illness or substance abuse
- physical, sexual or emotional abuse and neglect
- socio-economic difficulties
- homelessness
- discrimination.

The following sections highlight how some risk factors within the family and environment can impact on mental health and behaviour. However, the 'Five step framework' encourages us to be curious about all the risk factors that may be present.

Using the case studies

The purpose of the case studies is to highlight some of the risk factors that can impact on mental health and behaviour. However, it is important to remember that the presence of risk factors does not necessarily lead to mental health problems, but that awareness of risk factors and warning signs can help inform early identification and support. As such, the case studies are not intended to be used as a diagnostic tool, but to provide examples of using a five step framework when considering behavioural concerns.

The children in the case studies don't exist but reflect some of the typical concerns shared in consultations. Please note that the consultation questions were worked through over a series of sessions.

Disrupted early care

Case study: Shaheen, Year 1

Consultation process overview

Following the five step framework

STEP 1. **What can we see?** The first step is to summarise the concerns about Shaheen's progress, starting with a description of her behaviour, and thinking about how often it occurs, how long it lasts and where it usually happens.

STEP 2. **What have we tried?** Reflecting on the strategies and interventions already tried in school, and their impact.

STEP 3. **What do we know?** Bringing together what we already know about Shaheen. In order to consider a wider perspective, this includes incorporating Shaheen's own views and the views of those who know her best, such as her family, as well as looking at information held in school.

STEP 4. **What is the mental health message?** Reflecting on what we understand about Shaheen's difficulties, thinking about risk factors and warning signs, to consider a link between mental health and behaviour. Can we identify or predict any emerging mental health problems?

STEP 5. **What would personalised planning look like for Shaheen?** Finally, in light of this understanding how can we best support her? How can we strengthen protective factors for mental health and implement targeted mental health support?

Step 1: What can we see?

◯ What her teachers say...

Shaheen is one of the quieter, more independent children in class. She's always happiest doing her own thing. In Reception we didn't have any concerns – her behaviour didn't stand out so much and we thought she was a shy, sensitive little girl who needed some time to gain her confidence. However, now she is in Year 1 her behaviour seems more than childhood shyness, and we are worried that she is becoming increasingly detached and isolated from what is going on around her.

Most of the time Shaheen is very quiet and unassuming – it can be quite easy to forget she is there at all. But recently we have become aware of some more worrying aspects of her behaviour. For instance, Shaheen often appears disinterested in many of the classroom activities and responds with, what I can only describe as a 'blank' expression. At times this disinterest can be really visible, especially when compared to the excited and often loud reactions of her classmates. In fact, I am not sure I have ever seen Shaheen show much spontaneous joy or excitement. She can't seem to let herself go.

In class, Shaheen likes to do her own thing. At choosing time she will usually keep herself busy by, for instance, tidying the book corner, sharpening pencils, or sweeping the art area. We have noticed that she often prefers to choose activities that she can do on her own. She does interact with the other children – it's not as if she can't interact with them – but it is more a case that she often chooses not to. She particularly enjoys being helpful, and always likes to have a special job at tidy up time. However this can also cause problems, as she uses these 'jobs' to avoid group time. She often needs several reminders to rejoin the group.

Recently this avoidance has become more widespread. Shaheen is now increasingly reluctant to try anything new or unfamiliar. When we are introducing a new activity in class, she hangs back and doesn't engage. She will find any reason to avoid new tasks, such as saying she can't find something, needs to go to the toilet or tidy up. She takes a long time to find the confidence to try new things – it's almost as if she is so afraid of getting something wrong that she'd rather not try at all. This can be quite frustrating as she is more than capable of learning, but is really at risk of not achieving her potential.

She is an able girl who doesn't have any learning difficulties, and we have no worries about her academic progress. However, recently there have been a couple of occasions when we have found her work crumpled up in her tray. She always denies she has put it there and tries to blame other children. We can't understand why she is doing this – it's not as if we are giving her work that is too difficult or challenging.

We have also become aware that Shaheen has taken small items from the classroom without permission, for example, we suspect that she has taken things from the teacher's desk. Again, she denies any knowledge of this, even when we have found missing items in her pocket or when other children have seen her take things. The things she has taken are incidental and of no value: a packet of tissues, a pencil, or a hole punch. Shaheen sticks to her story and will say she didn't do it and it's as if she really believes what she says.

At break time she plays outside with the other children. At times she can be rather cautious, hanging back and watching the others carefully before joining in, but at other times she follows their lead and does things she knows to be inappropriate, such as running out of the playground to retrieve a ball which had been kicked on to the road – even though all children know that leaving the playground is strictly forbidden. When we asked her why she did this, she said that the others told her to. We find her behaviour so puzzling; on the one hand we have a young girl who is independent, cautious, quiet and seems to weigh everything up, yet on the other hand we have a young girl who can be very easily led and does things without thinking, such as stealing, lying and breaking rules. It just doesn't fit.

Shaheen does seem happier when she can predict what is going to happen, and on occasion she has appeared rather anxious when we have had changes to the classroom routine, for example, when we had visitors in school and the assembly time was changed. She didn't become *overly distressed like one of our autistic children, but she did seem even more reticent and unsure, and hung back until she was more confident about what was happening.*

Step 2: What have we tried?

⌕ What her teachers say. . .

Shaheen is a very able little girl, and we don't think she has any difficulties with her learning. At first we wondered about possible speech, language and communication needs because of her quiet and withdrawn behaviour, so we carried out some observations and assessments with her and also referred her for initial speech and language therapy assessment. The speech and language therapist confirmed that she doesn't have any underlying speech and language needs.

For a while we also wondered whether Shaheen could be somewhere on the autism spectrum. There were a few things about her behaviour that raised this question, for example, the way she hangs back, is quiet and sometimes worried by change. So we asked the speech and language therapist to think about this as well and to consider whether she needed further referral. The speech and language therapist didn't think Shaheen needed further referral as there are so many things about her that don't fit with an autism diagnosis. For example, although Shaheen prefers predictability, she doesn't rely on routines and sameness. Similarly, although she can be unsettled by change, she is usually quickly reassured. Shaheen often chooses to carry out activities alone but she can also be very sociable and interact with others. She also enjoys imaginative and pretend play with her friends when she chooses, and doesn't play in a restricted or repetitive way.

We have tried offering Shaheen rewards for good behaviour and work, for example when she completes a piece of work well, or when she tells the truth. We try to catch her being good and use various reward charts with her. However this hasn't been very successful, as she doesn't seem motivated by praise and reward – in fact, at times she seems to find it very difficult to accept. We found one of the charts torn up and hidden in her school bag.

When Shaheen has taken objects or items from others, we spend some time talking to her about it and trying to get her to understand that this is not acceptable behaviour. However, Shaheen always denies she has done anything wrong, and we almost begin to doubt ourselves. Since we haven't actually caught her in the act, it is a very difficult situation.

Step 3: What do we know?

🗐 Summary of key information from Shaheen's school file

* Shaheen had some involvement from the speech and language therapist when she was in Reception. The speech and language therapist suggested that her speech and language skills were at an age appropriate level. The therapist reported that Shaheen

was a shy and reticent young girl who would benefit from sensitive support to engage with others, initially in small group situations to build her confidence and self-esteem, and to experience lots of praise and reward.

- Shaheen's teacher assessments all indicate that she is working within the expected age range.

- Staff queried the possibility of autism because of Shaheen's preference for routine and familiarity. They liaised with the speech and language therapist about their concerns and initial investigations ruled this out.

- Shaheen was removed from her mother's care at the age of two under a voluntary care order, as her mother said she could no longer cope. She continues to have some contact with her mother, but this is irregular due to her mother's mental health issues. Her mother continues to have treatment for mental health and addiction issues.

- Shaheen lives with her maternal grandmother who is her main carer.

What her carer says. . .

Shaheen has lived with me for almost four years now. She usually sees her mum a couple of times a month, but this depends on how her mum is feeling at the time. Sometimes her mum is too ill to see her. Shaheen doesn't seem particularly bothered or upset by this, as long as we let her know beforehand. All in all, she copes quite well. She doesn't ever cry for her mum or talk that much about her. I think she was so young when she came to live with me that she doesn't really remember how it used to be when she lived with her mum – it's just the way it is for her now.

I describe Shaheen as, 'a little old woman'. She knows what she likes and what she doesn't. At home she likes to stick to what she knows. At bedtime we do more or less the same things each night: pyjamas, warm milk and toast, five minutes on the iPad then bed. It's the same when she gets home from school – we always do the same sort of thing. She can get quite upset when her routines change and that is the only time that she can get annoyed with me.

Shaheen likes to play with her cousins and her friends in the street. I am not aware of any problems other than the usual childish arguments about sharing and being nice to each other. I know they are getting a bit worried about her in school. They are worried that she is too quiet and afraid of trying new things. They say this might affect her progress. But she is a bright little girl. She loves stories and reading at home, and she likes to play with her dolls and cuddly toys. Shaheen has been through a lot in her young life and I just want things to be right for her. I'll do whatever I can to help her.

What Shaheen says. . .

Shaheen was encouraged to think of words and pictures to share her views, and what she wants others to know about her. She found it easier to draw pictures to show, 'the kind of girl she likes to be and 'doesn't like to be,' as a starting point for thinking about some of the things that help her. Encouraging Shaheen to think about the things that are important to her can support the development of self-awareness. This information was shared with other adults, with Shaheen's permission.

I like to be a girl who . . .

- Helps others
- Is kind and nice
- Smiles
- Does things well
- Can do lots of jobs
- Is clever
- Gets things right.

I don't like to be a girl who . . .

- Gets in trouble
- Gets things wrong
- Looks sad.

I like it best when . . .

- I know what is going to happen next
- I know what I have to do and why
- I have my own special jobs to do.

Step 4: What is the mental health message?

Given what we now know about Shaheen, can we identify any emerging mental health challenges, or an increased vulnerability of developing mental health problems? What are the risk factors and warning signs?

Key points from the consultations

- Shaheen's withdrawn and avoidant behaviour is becoming more apparent in school.
- She is reluctant to try new activities and tasks and hangs back from new challenges.
- She can interact with the other children but often appears to choose not to, preferring to do her own thing.

- Sometimes she can be easily led and does things that other children tell her to do.
- She has been accused of taking things from others, but she denies this when asked.
- She is not motivated by praise or reward.
- She prefers predictability and routine.
- She is doing well academically, and has no speech and language difficulties. Her difficulties are not thought to be part of an autism spectrum disorder.
- She has lived with her maternal grandmother since the age of two.
- Her mother has mental health and addiction problems.
- Shaheen says she likes to be kind and helpful, get things right and have special jobs to do. She doesn't like getting things wrong and prefers it when she is clear about what she has to do or what is going to happen next.

Could her behaviour reflect any emerging mental health problems?

Emerging mental health problems – risk factors and warning signs

1. Withdrawn and avoidant behaviour

Shaheen's withdrawn and avoidant behaviour is becoming more apparent as she gets older, and could indicate emerging mental health issues. School staff have monitored Shaheen's behaviour since Reception. They know that some children may be quieter and more anxious when they start school until they gain more skills and confidence. However, Shaheen's withdrawal is worsening and no longer seems to be developmentally appropriate. Some of her behaviour could be described as anxious. Children can feel anxious for a number of reasons, sometimes because of learning difficulties or disabilities, communication needs or perhaps due to traumatic events or their early experiences. School staff have considered the possibility of these factors and don't think she has any communication or learning needs. However, we know from school information, and from her gran, that Shaheen has had a disrupted early childhood. Sometimes children who have experienced disrupted parenting can display behaviour linked to insecure attachment, and Shaheen's avoidant and withdrawn behaviour may indicate attachment difficulties.

2. Disruption to early childhood

The disruption to Shaheen's early childhood is a risk factor for mental health problems. Although we don't know all of the details, we know that she was removed from her mother's care at the age of two. It is likely that Shaheen's experience of early parenting has been disrupted and disordered. She may not have had the opportunity to establish a close, nurturing relationship with her main caregiver in her early years. Even though she was placed in her gran's care at the age of two, we know that disrupted caregiving in infancy can have a long lasting impact on how children relate to others, and how they understand relationships and emotions. If Shaheen's mother was unable to attune and respond to Shaheen's basic emotional needs, then Shaheen may have learned to be mistrustful and rejecting of those around her. She may avoid approaching adults for help because she has learned that they are often unreliable.

3. Parental mental health and addiction problems

We know that parental mental health issues can be a risk factor for mental health problems in childhood, and can impact on parenting ability and consequent attachment behaviour and social and emotional development. Mental illness and addiction problems can make a parent less available to offer their child comfort and safety, and to respond sensitively to their needs. If a parent is less responsive to the needs of their child, this can be associated with childhood difficulties including lower self-esteem, lack of self-confidence, lower resilience and difficulties with social and emotional understanding and interactions.

4. Difficulties establishing and understanding relationships

Shaheen appears to be struggling to establish positive relationships with other children; sometimes she avoids their company and at other times she can be easily led. It may be that Shaheen is willing to do what others tell her in an effort to fit in, as she is struggling to understand social relationships.

Shaheen has also told us that it is important to her to be perceived as being 'good' at things, yet she doesn't always accept praise. Praise may be overwhelming for her and could also reflect her confusion about relationships and the reliability of others.

Conclusion

We recognise that Shaheen's behaviour could reflect underlying mental health challenges and there are several risk factors that increase her vulnerability. Therefore staff should consider personalised approaches to support Shaheen that take these factors into account.

Step 5: What would personalised planning look like for Shaheen?

Whole school approaches and systems

A personalised approach would need to consider whole school approaches and systems to support Shaheen, including:

- Shaheen's ongoing assessment needs – to ensure she is meeting her learning potential, and to monitor her withdrawal, anxiety and social and emotional development.

- How pastoral support can help Shaheen, exploring the need for counselling and key person support.

- A clear monitoring and review system. Staff will need to review the impact of any early support offered in school and agree triggers which would indicate the need for referral to others services. This could include referral to CAMHS, or educational psychology, for further social, emotional and mental health support, or to explore possible attachment issues.

- How information will be shared with school staff and the family about her progress and ongoing needs.

Protective factors for good mental health and resilience

As well as supporting mental health challenges, a personalised approach would build on protective factors for good mental health and resilience (see Chapter 2). Protective factors for good mental health include:

- The ability to understand and recognise one's own emotions, as well as the emotions of others, and to manage one's emotions in a socially acceptable way

- Having good peer influences and relationships in order to feel safe to discuss issues and practise social problem-solving

- Experiencing success and achievement

- Experiencing positive relationships with adults in school who can model a trusting, nurturing relationship and provide a secure, reliable base.

Therefore, a personalised approach for Shaheen would include strategies to support her emotional awareness and regulation, as well as promoting a sense of security and belonging. A key protective factor for Shaheen will be enabling her to experience trusting and consistent relationships in school.

Some specific strategies and approaches to support Shaheen's individual needs include:

1. Helping Shaheen to develop nurturing relationships with others

This could be achieved by:

- Providing a key person for Shaheen in school who can develop a consistent, trusting and nurturing relationship with her, and who can model sensitivity to Shaheen's emotional and social needs. Provide opportunities for Shaheen to check in with her key person throughout the day. One of the main aims of a key person is to promote a sense of belonging, connectedness and security.

- Providing opportunities for Shaheen to develop positive peer relationships. For example, offer small group work with a focus on promoting positive relationships and empathy, and exploring peer support systems such as buddying or circle of friends support. (See 'Circle of friends,' below.)

- Building on what is important to Shaheen by offering opportunities for her to have pre-agreed special 'jobs', such as helping in a younger class.

Circle of friends

The circle of friends approach originated in North America as an inclusion strategy which focuses on harnessing peer support, through encouraging understanding of the target child's individual needs. It involves sharing and explaining the needs of the target child, and facilitating a 'circle of friends' who meet together to find ways of supporting each other.

Setting up a circle of friends follows different stages, including meeting with the class to introduce the approach, to discuss the target child's challenges, and to elicit volunteers to make up the 'circle'. The circle of friends and the target child meet regularly to set goals and to discuss how to support each other, facilitated by an adult. This approach needs to be carefully managed and involves explaining the process to the target child and their parents/carers, and seeking their consent.

For further reading, see *Circles of friends. An inclusive approach to meeting emotional and behavioural difficulties, Newton Taylor and Wilson, 2007.* Or for an alternative way to implement this approach without naming the target child, see *A circle of friends approach with socially neglected children, Shotton, 2007.*

2. Helping Shaheen to develop her confidence and sense of security

This could be achieved by:

- Remembering to provide tasks that are achievable, with a careful balance of challenge and risk and broken into small manageable steps.

- Keeping praise in the here and now and focused on the task – give specific task-focused praise to reduce the emphasis on the relationship, for example say, 'That's neat handwriting today,' rather than, 'Good girl, I am pleased with the way you have done your handwriting today.' This shifts the focus from the person and relationship, to the activity.

- Encouraging Shaheen to use a personal visual timetable to help structure her day and provide predictability.

- If there is a planned change to the classroom routine or staff, prepare Shaheen for this beforehand, and reassure her that her key person will pop in to check how things are going.

- Building on Shaheen's desire to be helpful, ask her to do a job, such as looking after a particular item, when the teacher is not in class.

- Supporting transitions, as change and uncertainty may be particularly challenging for Shaheen. For example, offer additional emotional support during transition periods and use practical visual strategies, such as timetables, to help prepare for change.

- Creating an environment whereby making mistakes is accepted as part of the learning process. Model making mistakes of your own and demonstrate how this can help learning.

- Avoiding rejection or shame if there is a need to manage inappropriate behaviour – remain assertive, calm and warm. If Shaheen needs time out, try to avoid sending her out of the classroom if at all possible, and think of positive ways to reframe her behaviour.

3. Supporting her emotional awareness and emotional regulation

This could be achieved by:

- Helping her to build up a picture of her feelings by recognising and naming her emotions and wondering aloud what she might be feeling and why. For example say, 'I can see you are frowning right now. I wonder if you are worried because you are finding this activity a bit tricky? I wonder if we can break this activity down into very small steps?'

- Offering ways of regulating difficult emotions. For example, make a calm box with her with small items and objects she has chosen to help her manage her emotions – this could include colouring activities, stress balls, favourite books and stories, headphones and music etc. Model how she might use her calm box, saying, 'I can see you look a little upset, I wonder if you need a few minutes before rejoining the group. Let's look in your calm box and choose an activity together for a couple of minutes.' (See Louise Bomber, *Inside I'm hurting* for more information on the use of calm boxes.)

- Using role play and stories to help her extend her emotional vocabulary and to understand what others may be thinking and feeling.

- Remembering to communicate with her at her emotional age rather than her chronological age.

At a glance. . .

Disrupted early care

- Withdrawn, avoidant behaviour can be a sign of anxiety and stress and may be linked to insecure attachment. This can occur when a child has experienced adverse early experiences, such as disrupted or disordered care.

- Children with insecure attachment can present with a range of behaviours, this includes withdrawn and avoidant behaviour, as well as more visible confrontational, attention-seeking, unpredictable and acting out behaviour.

- Some children who have experienced their caregiver as unavailable and insensitive to their needs, may continue to fear rejection and so avoid approaching adults for support or help. These children may prefer to be self-reliant and have difficulty trusting others and asking for help. They may prefer to focus on the task rather than their relationship with others, and may be afraid of risking failure.

- Support for children with avoidant, withdrawn behaviour should focus on developing nurturing relationships, security and emotional awareness and regulation.

- It is important to consider allocating a key person who can develop a positive relationship with the child, work at the child's emotional age, and develop trust and security.

- When working with a child who may have experienced disrupted early care and whose behaviour is withdrawn and avoidant, remember to:

  ○ Support emotional awareness by building up a picture of feelings – recognise and name emotions, and wonder aloud what the child might be feeling and why.

  ○ Support emotional regulation by suggesting and modelling self-calming activities.

  ○ Provide tasks that are achievable, with a careful balance of challenge and risk, and broken into small manageable steps.

  ○ Keep praise in the here and now and focused on the task.

  ○ Increase structure and predictability by using visual strategies such as visual timetables, personal diaries and preparing carefully for any planned changes.

 'Think about children you know who present as withdrawn and insecure, and some of the factors that could be underpinning their behaviour.'

Trauma and neglect

Case study: Dan, Year 3

Consultation process overview

Following the five step framework

STEP 1. **What can we see?** The first step is to summarise the concerns about Dan's progress, starting with a description of his behaviour, and thinking about how often it occurs, how long it lasts and where it usually happens.

STEP 2. **What have we tried?** Reflecting on the strategies and interventions already tried in school, and their impact.

STEP 3. **What do we know?** Bringing together what we already know about Dan. In order to consider a wider perspective, this includes incorporating Dan's own views and the views of those who know him best, such as his family, as well as looking at information held in school.

STEP 4. **What is the mental health message?** Reflecting on what we understand about Dan's difficulties, thinking about risk factors and warning signs, to consider a link between mental health and behaviour. Can we identify or predict any emerging mental health problems?

STEP 5. **What would personalised planning look like for Dan?** Finally, in light of this understanding how can we best support him? How can we strengthen protective factors for mental health and implement targeted mental health support?

Step 1: What can we see?

⟲ What his teachers say. . .

Dan's behaviour is unpredictable and disruptive on a daily basis. He was removed from his parents' care while in nursery and he is now in his third foster care placement. Information about his early years is sketchy, but we do know that Dan was slightly premature and required some special care after his birth. We also understand that the family had a lot of involvement from social care as his father was deemed a risk because of his offending behaviour. We believe this involved violence and physical abuse, but we don't know the details. We have been told that Dan suffered some neglect in his early years and that his mother was alcohol dependent during the pregnancy. Dan was eventually placed in his first foster care placement when he was three years old. He no longer has any contact with his parents and social services are seeking permanent adoption.

His first two foster placements broke down because of his unpredictable and difficult behaviour. All of his placements have been local so that Dan can stay at this school. However, we know that this latest placement is not going well and the carers are unsure if they can manage him longer term. We are experiencing the same problems in school.

Dan's behaviour can be quite provocative in that he seeks out challenge and creates arguments. He will challenge adults by questioning their direction and swearing and name calling when he doesn't agree with them or doesn't want to do something. Most of the challenging situations occur during unstructured situations such as break time and lunchtime, because of his difficulties interacting with the other children. He wants to interact and play with the others but Dan has great difficulty managing the usual ups and downs of friendships and social interactions. Seemingly minor incidents and comments become magnified and quickly escalate into major situations. He seems to take things very personally, and can't move on from incidents and will sometimes hold a grudge for several days. Dan usually responds to minor disputes by going into fight mode; he has very little tolerance of others and will become quickly defensive. We have had many complaints from other parents about Dan's behaviour and his negative influence on their own children.

Dan can sometimes appear quite single-minded. He can't understand how his behaviour makes other people feel, and he shows very little empathy with them. His responses can be unpredictable and explosive, so the other children are understandably quite wary of him. He will regularly respond with anger and frustration when he can't get his own way.

Unsurprisingly Dan is struggling with work in class. He is now working well below age expected levels and the gap is widening between him and his peers.

In the classroom he is highly demanding of adult attention: he is often out of his seat looking for the teacher or assistant, he will talk over others with little respect for the need to take his turn and share adult attention, and he will snatch equipment and resources. When he is unable to get attention or his own way, he will lash out verbally or physically. It is really difficult to think of anything that is going well for Dan at the moment, as each day seems to be dominated by his behaviour challenges.

All in all, Dan's behaviour detracts from the classroom teaching. He often creates chaos and mayhem in the classroom and we are left to deal with the aftermath, in which Dan is often angry and defensive and others around him are upset and disrupted. We know that Dan has suffered a lot of change in his family life, and his new placement is now under threat. Dan's own behaviour seems to sabotage any chance of a settled placement, and this is now having an impact on the education of the other children in the class.

Step 2: What have we tried?

ℚ What his teachers say...

We know that Dan needs clear boundaries and sanctions to give him a sense of security and we have always been very clear with him about what is acceptable behaviour and what is not. However, he constantly challenges the boundaries and doesn't comply with sanctions. On occasion, behavioural incidents have escalated to such an extent that we have needed to use physical restraint or exclusion from the classroom to the headteacher's office. When this happens, Dan will eventually calm down and be able to go back to the classroom. However, he doesn't appear to learn from these interventions and there have been occasions where he has returned to the classroom apparently calm, only for his behaviour to escalate again within minutes of his return. We know Dan has significant emotional difficulties, but it is important that other children see us applying the same behaviour strategies and rules that we apply to them. We don't want to be seen to be condoning his behaviour.

We were advised by the behaviour support team to try buddying him with a group of children in the playground. However, this inevitably ends with Dan challenging something they have said or done, resulting in tears and tantrums. His interactions with the other children are a particular area of concern and we don't think it is fair on the other children to place this responsibility on them. Most of the children are reluctant to include him in their games as they say Dan always spoils them.

We referred Dan to our Educational Psychologist (EP) last year for some advice about his learning, and ideas for support. The EP told us that his thinking and learning skills fell well below the average range, and that he had particular difficulty with verbal reasoning and problem-solving tasks. The EP suggested that we use visual support strategies in the classroom to support his verbal reasoning and understanding, and that he needs a differentiated curriculum with a small step approach to learning. He also suggested further investigation and paediatric referral into the nature of his developmental difficulties. However, because of the frequent change in his foster care placements, I don't think this has happened yet.

Step 3: What do we know?

🗐 Summary of key information from Dan's school file

- Dan has been looked after in foster care from the age of three.
- There is a history of abuse and neglect, and his mother was alcohol dependent during pregnancy.
- Dan required special care after his birth and there are concerns on file about the level of alcohol consumption during pregnancy and possible effects on his development.
- A permanent adoption is being sought, and two foster care placements have broken down due to difficulties managing his behaviour.
- The behaviour support team has been involved as well as the Educational Psychologist. The Educational Psychologist's report noted cognitive skills within the below average range, with particular concerns about his verbal reasoning and

problem-solving. This refers to his ability to solve problems using words and to process verbal information to make sense of it.

- Educational psychology recommendations included close monitoring and referral for paediatric/CAMHS overview to consider effects of early trauma on his development.

ℚ What his foster carers say...

Dan has been with us now for almost six months. We know it is still early days, but nevertheless we are increasingly worried about his behaviour and the impact on our wider family. We don't have any other youngsters with us at the moment as everyone felt that Dan needed our full attention and would find it difficult to share our time with any other children. However, we still have our wider family, nieces, nephews and friends and we are finding it increasingly difficult to socialise and engage with them because of Dan's unpredictable behaviour.

We feel as if Dan is constantly testing the boundaries on a daily basis, and it is extremely tiring. Although we have put clear routines and structure in place at home, he questions and challenges and tries to create arguments about every little thing. It is very difficult to remain calm at times. When we have family or friends around he is extremely attention-seeking and tries to play one person off against the other. When he is told, 'no', he will often have a tantrum – shout, yell, swear and scream until he tires himself out. It can be extremely embarrassing. We know we have to be consistent and can't give in to his every demand, but it is exhausting.

On a more positive note, when Dan is the focus of our attention we can have some very good days. He loves going to the cinema with us and he likes to go swimming and to the soft play area. We do have to be careful to manage his play. We find that if we leave him to his own devices to play with the other children it will always end in trouble! We literally need to be by his side helping him play nicely and not to overreact. When we do this, we find he can be much more engaging, and the experience can be much more positive.

We are worried about his learning. It has been highlighted that he is behind other children of the same age and this isn't helping him to fit in at school. We do wonder what else we can do to help him and keep him with us.

ℚ What Dan says...

Dan enjoyed spending time with a learning mentor to talk about his likes and dislikes. He was happy for the adult to write down his words to record his views. This encouraged Dan to focus on his strengths and challenges and to think about how others can best help him, as well as how he can help himself. This information was then written into a personal profile, which Dan agreed could be shared with other adults in his life.

Dan's personal profile

Things that are important to me

- Having my transformers in my bedroom with me so I can play with them before bedtime.
- Going to see films with Ann and Frank and getting salty popcorn to eat.
- Watching my TV programmes when I get in from school.
- Being allowed to play football at playtime.

Things I find difficult

- Nothing much, except sometimes I find spellings and maths tricky.
- Not being allowed to play football.

Things you need to know about me

- I don't like gravy on my dinners.
- Sometimes I get mad and I always end up crying and I don't know why I cry.
- I like to play football because I am good at it.

Step 4: What is the mental health message?

Given what we now know about Dan, can we identify any emerging mental health challenges, or an increased vulnerability of developing mental health problems? What are the risk factors and warning signs?

Key points from the consultations

- Dan has been looked after in foster care since the age of three due to parental neglect.
- His mother consumed high levels of alcohol during pregnancy.
- He has a history of failed foster care placements due to difficulties managing his behaviour.
- In school, his behaviour is described as attention-seeking and unpredictable. He will challenge adults by questioning their direction, swearing and name calling when he doesn't agree with them or doesn't want to do something. He can be physically aggressive.
- He has particular difficulties sustaining positive relationship with his peers, especially during unstructured play.

- He has some difficulties learning, especially in the areas of verbal reasoning and problem-solving.
- His carers describe his behaviour as attention-seeking and prone to tantrums.
- His carers note he can play alongside other children when supported by an adult.
- Dan says that he likes playing football, watching his favourite TV programmes and going to the cinema with his foster carers.
- He expresses some confusion about why he feels angry and upset.

Could his behaviour reflect any emerging mental health problems?

Emerging mental health problems – risk factors and warning signs

1. Early childhood trauma

Dan's early experiences of trauma, including exposure to neglectful and abusive parenting, his mother's alcohol consumption while pregnant, and loss and separation, all place Dan at increased risk of mental health problems. Trauma can include exposure to events such as disasters and accidents, as well as exposure to hostile or rejecting relationships including abuse, bullying or domestic violence. In such traumatic circumstances children may have experienced very high levels of exposure to the stress hormone, cortisol. This can result in over-activation of the stress response so that children may appear on constant high alert, causing them to react as if they are under serious threat for relatively minor incidents. In addition, exposure to early childhood trauma can also affect the structure of the developing brain, meaning that children exposed to traumatic experiences and adverse care may find it more difficult to problem-solve, direct attention, concentrate, and develop social and emotional understanding.

Children who are exposed to loss or separation are at increased risk of mental health problems. Loss and separation can include loss experienced through being taken to live elsewhere or into care, as well as bereavement, family conflict or friendship losses. Looked-after children experience significant loss, and are at increased risk of mental health problems. A paper by Sempik, Ward and Darker in 2008, which looked at children who remained in care for at least a year, found that 72% had mental health or behavioural problems. Dan has experienced disrupted and neglectful early parenting experiences, as well as failed foster care placements, which all place him at increased risk of mental health issues.

In addition, Dan's exposure to alcohol during pregnancy may have had an impact on his cognitive development and problem-solving ability. We know that foetal exposure to alcohol can have a significant effect on the developing brain, and that these effects can continue through life. Dan has been identified as having some cognitive challenges and is working at a level below his chronological age. In order to understand this fully, it will be useful to seek further medical advice.

2. Behaviour linked to insecure attachment

Dan's behaviour may reflect significant attachment difficulties. Some children who have experienced trauma and neglect, demonstrate behaviour linked to insecure attachment. According to the NICE guidelines, *Children's attachment: final scope*, 'Around 80% of children who suffer maltreatment are classified as having disorganised attachment.' These children may appear to be on high alert most of the time, easily distracted with a strong sense of fear, panic or helplessness. Their behaviour may be extremely difficult to manage and may appear bizarre, extreme, unpredictable and distressing to those around them. This kind of attachment difficulty can be linked with social and cognitive problems.

Dan's tantrum-like behaviour may reflect a search for boundaries and security, similar to that of a younger child during the 'terrible twos'. His attention-seeking and hyperactive behaviour may be linked to difficulties understanding and trusting that adults will meet his needs. His early care giving experiences may have taught him that adults are unpredictable and unreliable, and consequently he may have had little experience of having his emotions understood and contained. Dan's attention-seeking and hyper-vigilant behaviour may be his way of ensuring he receives adult attention.

3. Learning challenges

Dan's learning challenges are also a risk factor for mental health problems. His limited verbal reasoning and problem-solving skills may be contributing to social and interaction difficulties, as well as affecting his self-esteem, confidence and positive perception of himself as a learner.

Conclusion

There are multiple risk factors for mental health problems present in Dan's life. While we know that the presence of risk factors does not necessarily mean children will go on to develop mental health problems, we also know that a greater number of risk factors increases the likelihood of experiencing difficulties. Therefore staff should consider personalised approaches to support Dan that take these factors into account.

Step 5: What would personalised planning look like for Dan?

Whole school approaches and systems

A personalised approach would need to consider whole school approaches and systems to support Dan including:

- Dan's ongoing assessment needs and how staff will monitor and measure his progress and have clear triggers and mechanisms for referring to other services, including paediatric and CAMHS support.

- Building in multi-agency reviews so that information and advice can be shared with school staff and social care, and support for his foster carers can be coordinated.
- How the pastoral system can support Dan, including seeking counselling support.
- The need for school staff training and development to help them understand and manage the impact of traumatic early experiences and attachment difficulties in school.
- Whole school approaches to support behaviour management that focus on a relational framework, with an emphasis on understanding and managing emotions in response to behaviour challenges.

Protective factors for good mental health and resilience

As well as supporting mental health challenges, a personalised approach would build on protective factors for positive mental health and resilience (see Chapter 2, page 17). Protective factors for good mental health include:

- Being able to communicate with other children and adults and engage socially
- Having support for educational and learning needs
- Having a sense of belonging and experiencing trusting relationships in school
- Feeling safe to raise and discuss problems.
- Experiencing success and achievement.

Therefore, a personalised approach for Dan would include strategies to support his problem-solving and reasoning skills, as well as thinking about how to promote his feelings of safety and predictability in school, and the development of reliable and responsive relationships.

Some specific strategies and approaches to support Dan's individual needs include:

1. Developing responsive and reliable relationships

This could be achieved by:

- Assigning a key person to take on the role of a positive, caring and protective adult who can be a point of contact in school to provide reassurance and structure for Dan.
- Providing opportunities for the key person to facilitate positive interactions with other children through modelling interactions and talking through any challenges as they occur.
- Helping Dan to understand that he will be 'held in mind' by his key person. For example, give him small objects to look after, or remind him, 'I will be wondering how you are in your literacy lesson and I will look forward to talking to you about it this afternoon'.
- Ensuring staff understand the nature of Dan's difficulties and the impact of his early experiences on his behaviour.

2. Increasing predictability

This could be achieved by:

- Paying particular attention to beginnings and endings of lessons, and establishing some reliable routines.
- Using visual strategies such as personal timetables and diaries.
- Anticipating and planning for change whenever possible.
- Having clear, reliable and consistent boundaries in school, and clear and agreed strategies for responding to incidents. Encourage the key person to talk through any incidents with Dan, naming and noticing his emotions and reactions. Have some calming activities available and model their use.

3. Focusing on a relational framework, linking behaviour to understanding and management of emotions

This could be achieved by:

- Dealing with emotions 'in the moment' and before they escalate, whenever possible, and using incidents as opportunities to teach and build trusting and respectful relationships.
- Encouraging Dan to understand that we all experience 'good' and 'not so good' feelings as part and parcel of the challenges of everyday life, and helping him to notice and accept these feelings and emotions.
- Working with Dan to find out what helps him manage his 'not so good' feelings, and modeling how to use self-calming strategies.
- Trying to avoid 'time out' strategies as these may increase Dan's feelings of shame and rejection. If possible, try to 'bring him in' to sit at a quiet table closer to the adult, to minimise feelings of rejection and exclusion.

4. Supporting his learning challenges, problem-solving skills and positive perception of himself as someone who can achieve

This could be achieved by:

- Raising awareness of his strengths and incorporating his interests to develop his self-esteem.
- Encouraging Dan to engage in a range of extra-curricular activities so that experiences of success and achievement are not restricted to academic tasks.

- Providing structured support during play to enable positive relationships and promote social problem-solving in real-life situations.

- Seeking further staff support from other professionals to understand Dan's learning challenges and how best to support them.

At a glance...

Trauma and neglect

- Children exposed to early childhood trauma are at increased risk of mental health problems and can display highly disturbing and disorganised behaviour.

- Trauma can include exposure to events such as disasters and accidents, exposure to hostile or rejecting relationships including abuse, bullying or domestic violence, and loss or separation.

- When children experience trauma, they may be exposed to very high levels of the stress hormone, cortisol. This can result in over-activation of the stress response so that children may appear on constant high alert.

- Exposure to early childhood trauma can also have an impact on the developing brain, leading to increased difficulties problem-solving, directing attention and concentrating, and developing social and emotional understanding. Consequently this can impact on a child's ability to learn effectively and develop social and emotional skills.

- Children who have experienced trauma and neglect, loss and separation are at increased risk of mental health problems. This includes looked-after children. A study looking at children who remained in care for at least a year, found that 72% had mental health or behavioural problems, and 'around 80% of children who suffer maltreatment are classified as having disorganised attachment' (National Institute for Health and Care Excellence). This means their behaviour may be difficult to understand and manage, they may appear on high alert, attention seeking and demanding.

- When supporting children whose behaviour may be linked to trauma and neglect, remember to:

  - Focus on developing responsive and reliable relationships by assigning a key person who can model a positive relationship and help promote friendships in school.

  - Increase predictability and security by using visual strategies and thinking carefully about clear and consistent boundaries.

  - Think about managing behaviour by encouraging the child to better understand his and others' emotions. Use incidents as opportunities to teach and build trusting and respectful relationships.

- Help the child to find strategies that will help during times of stress and anxiety.
- Avoid behaviour management strategies that could increase the child's sense of shame and rejection.

 'Do staff in school understand the possible impact of childhood trauma and neglect?'

Inconsistent discipline and family breakdown

Case study: Cameron, Year 4

Consultation process overview

STEP 1. **What can we see?** The first step is to summarise the concerns about Cameron's progress, starting with a description of his behaviour, and thinking about how often it occurs, how long it lasts and where it usually happens.

STEP 2. **What have we tried?** Reflecting on the strategies and interventions already tried in school, and their impact.

STEP 3. **What do we know?** Bringing together what we already know about Cameron. In order to consider a wider perspective, this includes incorporating Cameron's own views and the views of those who know him best, such as his family, as well as looking at information held in school.

STEP 4. **What is the mental health message?** Reflecting on what we understand about Cameron's difficulties, thinking about risk factors and warning signs, to consider a link between mental health and behaviour. Can we identify or predict any emerging mental health problems?

STEP 5. **What would personalised planning look like for Cameron?** Finally, in light of this understanding how can we best support him? How can we strengthen protective factors for mental health and implement targeted mental health support?

Step 1: What can we see?

◯ What his teachers say. . .

Cameron's behaviour in school is becoming really challenging. He is defiant, questions authority and is incredibly argumentative. His behaviour is worse in the classroom and in situations where he has to follow rules and direction. He struggles to accept anyone telling him what to do – it can be extremely tiring for those around him. Sometimes it is as if he deliberately tries to challenge and upset others just for the sake of it! We regularly see outbursts of anger, swearing and name-calling. His behaviour can appear very toddler-like, with lots of testing of boundaries and pushing limits, and then throwing a temper tantrum when he doesn't get his own way.

On a bad day, Cameron can lose his temper several times. This usually happens when he is asked to do something he doesn't want to do. He is developing a real problem with accepting any requests or directions. A typical incident will begin with him verbally challenging instructions.

For example, if he doesn't want to do a particular thing, he will say something like, 'Why should I?' or 'I don't feel like it!' or 'I don't want to!' and put his head on the desk and pretend he is sleeping. When we insist that he complies, he will often insult the adult who is directing him. He will typically call them names, swear and comment on their appearance. Sometimes this can be very personal. He seems to know exactly which buttons to press.

More recently, his behaviour has become physical. He will charge around the classroom or he will hide and refuse to move. We give him warnings and tell him he must have some time out, but he usually challenges this, shouts, screams and swears until we need to use physical restraint.

Once he is removed from the classroom he is taken to a 'cool down' area, usually the head of pastoral care's office, if it is available. Typically he will shout and scream for a while, and on a couple of occasions he has tried to throw objects and has had to be further restrained. However, he usually calms down eventually, and will say when he is ready to go back to the classroom.

As you can imagine, these incidents are disruptive and draining. We feel we are treading on eggshells as we never really know when Cameron will blow his top. We are worried that his behaviour will escalate even more and we feel that we need to address it now before it becomes unmanageable.

We are aware that Cameron has some learning challenges; his work is differentiated accordingly and he works in a group that receives extra support. However, we have other children in his class with greater learning difficulties than Cameron, so we don't think his behaviour can be fully explained by his learning needs.

Unsurprisingly, Cameron's friendships with the other children in his class are strained. Cameron tends to blame others for things he has done, which does nothing to help his popularity. When other children are doing what he wants to do he can play well without any problems. However, he gets very easily annoyed when they don't do exactly what he wants. Then he will call them names and be unkind, saying quite mean things about them. Consequently, we are noticing that more often he is on his own at break time.

We know his mum is struggling with his behaviour at home. She often comes into school upset and frustrated, but we think that she gives in to him a lot of the time. We do have some sympathy with this because she is on her own and it is easier to give in and do what he wants. We know his behaviour can be very difficult and draining, and she doesn't always have the energy to deal with his demands. However, this inconsistency doesn't help us in school when we are trying to remain firm and consistent in our approach.

Step 2: What have we tried?

◯ What his teachers say...

We are working closely with Cameron's mum, and she has attended a parenting course at the local children's centre. She said it helped at first, but that his behaviour is still very difficult at home. We have regular meetings with her in school to discuss his behaviour and we are thinking about making a referral to the Child and Adolescent Mental Health Services (CAMHS), as we need advice about how to support him at home and in school.

We have given Cameron support for his learning needs. His work is carefully differentiated, and each morning he works in a small group for literacy and numeracy.

We are very clear with Cameron about our school rules and expectations, and we do try to reward his good behaviour, even though this is increasingly challenging. We have tried using star charts and breaking down rewards into small achievable steps, so that he is working for a reward of his choice at the end of the week. Sometimes this can start out positively, but Cameron will often say he is not bothered and it is 'stupid'. He sometimes refuses rewards and scorns them. We give clear warning and sanctions and use a traffic light system to help him understand when he is on a warning. Sanctions have included staying in at break time, going to the headteacher's office, having to work in the year 6 class and exclusions. Nothing seems to have a long-term impact.

Step 3: What do we know?

🗎 Summary of key information from Cameron's School file

- Cameron's general learning ability falls within the below average range.
- Previous assessment carried out by advisory support teachers and school staff suggests that literacy and numeracy are particularly challenging for him, and his auditory working memory is poor. This refers to his ability to remember and process spoken information.
- The behaviour intervention team has been involved, and has carried out some observations. They suggested strategies, including using a traffic light system to help reinforce clear warnings and sanctions, rewarding positive behaviour using star charts and positive reinforcement, and talking to his mother about a referral to CAMHS.
- His mother has attended a parenting group after sharing her worries about his behaviour at home.

⚲ What his mother says. . .

Cameron is a worry at the moment. I know his teachers are having the same problems with his behaviour as I am at home. I live alone with Cameron, as his dad and I split up three years ago. I was quite low after Cameron was born and was told I had postnatal depression. Cameron's dad wasn't much help in the early days and it took a long time before I began to feel better. When Cameron started school it made things a bit easier and I thought that things were just starting to get better – but then Cameron's dad left me. We don't have any contact with him any more as he moved away after our split, and I don't get any support at home. I have found the past few years really hard for many different reasons, and Cameron's behaviour has made this worse. I dread getting the phone calls from school telling me he has kicked off yet again.

I have tried everything with Cameron and nothing seems to work. At first I was probably a bit easy on Cameron because I felt guilty and sorry for him after his dad left, as I know Cameron missed him. Looking back, I probably gave in to Cameron too much when was he was younger, and perhaps spoiled him a bit. When I realised this wasn't any good for him I became much stricter and made sure there were consequences for his naughty behaviour, things like: taking away his computer, not letting him play out, and using a 'naughty step'. Nothing has seemed to work though. It's really hard to know what to do to get through to him and sometimes, I have to admit, he goes on at me so much I just give up because I don't know what else to do. I have been on a parenting course after talking to his teachers, but none of those ideas seem to work either.

Sometimes he can be a lovely little boy, especially when he's doing things he enjoys – it's sad that no one really sees that side of him anymore.

I am really struggling with him now and have had to go to the doctor, who has given me some medication for my nerves.

◯ What Cameron says. . .

In discussions with Cameron, he talked about things he enjoys but struggled to identify any difficulties or issues at home or at school. He put his head on the desk and said the questions were 'stupid'. However, he was able to draw a picture of himself and the things he would be doing on a 'good day' and on a 'bad day', which were then used to share Cameron's views.

On a good day. . .

- We do science experiments
- We go outside for PE
- I play outside at break time
- Everyone plays with me
- I do all of my work on the computer
- I have chips for lunch
- I am smiling.

On a bad day. . .

- People want me to do stupid things and I get angry
- Teachers shout
- We do literacy all day
- I have to stay in at break time
- No one lets me play
- I have carrots for lunch.

Step 4: What is the mental health message?

Given what we now know about Cameron, can we identify any emerging mental health challenges, or an increased vulnerability of developing mental health problems? What are the risk factors and warning signs?

Key points from the consultations

- There are significant concerns at home and at school about Cameron's defiant and oppositional behaviour. He struggles to accept authority and can lose his temper easily.
- His behavioural difficulties are having an impact on his progress in school.
- Cameron has some recognised learning challenges, particularly for literacy and numeracy skills, and auditory working memory difficulties.
- He receives additional support for his learning challenges.
- His behaviour has an impact on his peer relationships – the other children are wary of Cameron and often choose not to interact with him because of his behaviour.
- His mother says she is struggling with his behaviour at home and is taking medication for her 'nerves'. She also notes a period of postnatal depression.
- His mother acknowledges that her parenting has been inconsistent since Cameron's father left three years ago, and she is coping alone.
- Cameron likes practical lessons such as science and PE, and he likes to play outside.
- He dislikes literacy and having to stay in school at break time.
- He has difficulty recognising how his behaviour contributes to conflicts with other children.

Could his behaviour reflect any emerging mental health problems?

Emerging mental health problems – risk factors and warning signs

1. Change in behaviour

Cameron's behaviour is becoming increasingly challenging at home and at school. Cameron struggles to accept authority and his behaviour is described as defiant and argumentative. This behaviour is particularly apparent when he is asked to follow rules and direction. Problems of conduct, such as defiant, oppositional and antisocial behaviour, are the most common reasons for referral to child and adolescent mental health services. (National Institute for Health and Care Excellence (NICE) clinical guidelines). These guidelines also note that problems of conduct and behaviour are commonly associated with other difficulties, including learning problems, attention difficulties, social and interaction problems and additional mental health issues.

2. Inconsistent parenting and family breakdown

Cameron has experienced inconsistent parenting and family breakdown, and his mother may have ongoing, mental health issues.

When children experience inconsistent or harsh parenting, this can affect how they understand relationships, interact with others and behave. For example, they may become mistrustful of adults, lack security and want to maintain control. There are also other risk factors in the family and wider environment that can be associated with an increased risk of conduct problems. These include: parental mental health problems, such as parental depression, substance misuse, low family income and poverty, and living in high crime and antisocial communities.

Cameron's parents have separated and his mother acknowledges that her parenting has been inconsistent and that she is sometimes struggling to cope. She had postnatal depression and is currently taking medication 'for nerves'. All of these factors may increase Cameron's vulnerability of developing mental health problems.

3. Impact of behaviour on achievement and relationships

Cameron's behaviour is having an impact on his progress in school and his relationships with other children and adults. Problems of conduct and behaviour are commonly associated with other difficulties, including learning and achievement, and social and interaction problems. When children struggle to establish social relationships and friendships, this can lead to feelings of isolation or frustration. Difficulties achieving and succeeding in school can further increase a sense of 'not belonging' and difference. All of these factors can impact negatively on mental health.

4. Learning

Cameron's learning needs are a risk factor for mental health issues. His identified learning challenges include literacy and numeracy difficulties and working memory issues. We know that learning difficulties or disabilities can be a risk factor for mental health problems, for example, children with learning difficulties may become frustrated and annoyed when faced with tasks they find difficult – they may respond by opting out and refusing to work, and behavioural difficulties can be common. Although having a learning difficulty is not a mental health problem, living with a learning difficulty can increase the risk of low self-esteem, low self-worth and anxiety.

Conclusion

There are several factors in Cameron's life that could increase his risk of mental health issues, and there are several indicators to suggest that emerging mental health challenges underpin his current behaviour. His behaviour can be challenging and confrontational at home and at school, particularly when he is asked to follow direction. He also has some identified learning challenges, and is experiencing difficulties establishing social relationships with other children. Therefore staff should consider personalised approaches to support Cameron that take these factors into account.

Step 5: What would personalised planning look like for Cameron?

Whole school approaches and systems

A personalised approach would need to consider whole school approaches and systems to support Cameron, including:

- Cameron's ongoing assessment needs, including further understanding of his learning challenges, how to monitor and support his behaviour and social skills, and clear systems for knowing when to refer to other services.

- How the pastoral team can support Cameron, exploring the need for key worker and counselling support to model positive and warm adult relationships and to promote his resilience, self-esteem and understanding of his behaviour.

- How to maintain a positive and supportive relationship with Cameron's mother, offering multi-agency support, and supporting her own emotional and mental health needs.

Protective factors for good mental health and resilience

As well as supporting emerging mental health challenges, a personalised approach would build on protective factors for good mental health and resilience (see Chapter 2, page 17). These include:

- Being able to achieve and experience success in school, in extracurricular as well as curricular activities.

- Having a sense of belonging and positive peer relationships

- Having support for learning challenges

- Good home–school communication and support.

Therefore a personalised approach for Cameron would include strategies to support awareness and management of his behaviour, as well as thinking about how to prevent social isolation, ensure curriculum access, and how to help him develop a positive self-image.

Some specific strategies and approaches to support Cameron's individual needs include:

1. Having clear and consistent behavioural management strategies, which are shared with Cameron and consistently applied by all adults in school

This could be achieved by:

- Ensuring Cameron fully understands the consequences of appropriate and inappropriate behaviour by reinforcing strategies with visual and pictorial reminders.

- Giving clear and fixed choices, so that Cameron has some flexibility of choice within adult direction, e.g. 'Would you like to do the writing task using this new pencil or this fine tipped pen?'

- Considering using proactive support before Cameron's behaviour escalates by encouraging him to use a cool down or chill out area, or by engaging him in a task elsewhere, for example: redirecting him to a high interest activity, or asking him to take a message to the main office. Consider and agree when this strategy might be most useful and how the use of the cool down area or redirection can be linked to noticing, naming and managing his emotions

- Encouraging staff to be aware of the impact of their own emotions when dealing with behavioural incidents, for example: to think about body language and voice use; to try to portray calmness and control; keeping comments brief; and knowing when to seek additional support from colleagues!

2. Helping Cameron identify and manage his emotions, and gain awareness of others' emotions

This could be achieved by:

- Noticing, labelling and naming his emotions – note what may have triggered his reactions, and explore ways of managing his emotions together. When noticing and naming his emotions it may be helpful to adopt a stance of curiosity, e.g. 'I wonder if you are feeling anxious right now? I wonder if that could be because I asked you to do this piece of work?' This could help Cameron to become more aware of his emotions and when they are likely to occur.

- Encouraging Cameron to keep track of his emotions, the triggers and his consequent behaviour by keeping an 'emotions and triggers diary' (see below).

- Teaching Cameron how to say 'no' and refuse in a socially acceptable way.

Emotions and triggers diary

When supporting children to notice, name and manage their emotions it can be helpful to encourage them to keep a diary or a journal. Encouraging children to write or draw about their emotions in this way can provide a visual reminder to support their understanding, help them to identify triggers and think about ways of managing their emotions in the future.

Remember to explain that it is normal, and even helpful, to experience a range of emotions and that emotions can lead to 'good feelings' and 'not so good feelings'.

Encourage the child to record:

- The name of the emotion
- Where they noticed the emotion in their body, e.g. in their stomach, felt hot, felt tense. . .
- Whether this was a 'good feeling' or a 'not so good feeling'
- What happened before they felt the emotion
- What they were thinking
- What did they do?

As an extension activity, help the child to begin to identify what helps them to manage their emotions. For example, what could they do or think the next time they experience the emotion?

3. Promoting his interpersonal and friendship skills

This could be achieved by:

- Using small group work and circle time sessions to model and practise positive social and friendship skills, such as turn taking, listening and sharing.
- Using role play and drawing comic strips to understand situations that have caused conflict in school, with a particular focus on thoughts and feelings and how they can be linked to behaviour.
- Using small group work to practise stopping and thinking before responding, and how to express feelings and viewpoints in an acceptable way.

4. Supporting his individual learning needs, confidence and self-esteem

This could be achieved by:

- Identifying and supporting his learning challenges by providing suitably differentiated tasks.
- Presenting information visually using diagrams, pictures, and timetables to support his memory, and learning challenges.
- Using his personal strengths and interests to engage him in activities. Cameron particularly enjoys practical science activities, PE, computers and opportunities to play with others.
- Agreeing how best to praise and reward Cameron – previous reward strategies have had limited effect and he will often say he is, 'not bothered'. Consider keeping praise specific, in the here and now, and linked to effort rather than success. Cameron may

prefer a low-key approach such as writing a note of praise in his diary, giving a thumbs up sign, or receiving a praise card on his desk that can go towards receiving an agreed reward later.

At a glance. . .

Inconsistent discipline and family breakdown

- Problems of conduct, such as defiant, oppositional and antisocial behaviour, are the most common reasons for referral to child and adolescent mental health services. (National Institute for Health and Care Excellence (NICE) clinical guidelines).

- Some of the risk factors for developing conduct problems include poor, inconsistent or punitive experiences of care, parental mental health problems, living in poverty, and having low educational attainment. It is important to be aware of the presence of these risk factors in order to provide early support.

- Problems of conduct and behaviour are commonly associated with other difficulties, including: learning problems, attention difficulties, social and interaction problems and additional mental health issues (NICE clinical guidelines).

- When working with children who demonstrate oppositional, defiant behaviour remember to:

  - Provide opportunities to model positive, warm relationships with adults – think about doing this through allocating a key person and providing counselling in school.

  - Have clear and consistent behavioural management strategies that are shared with the child and consistently applied by all adults in school. Remember to give clear fixed choices and use proactive support to interrupt escalating behaviour by redirecting the child's attention or briefly removing the child from the situation by engaging them in a task elsewhere. Support staff should be aware of the impact of their own emotions when dealing with behavioural incidents.

  - Help them to identify and regulate their own emotions, and gain awareness of others' emotions. Think about noticing and naming emotions, for example, wonder aloud what may have triggered escalating emotions, and explore ways of managing emotions together. Link the use of a calm down area, or redirection activities to noticing and naming emotions. Encourage children to keep track of their own emotions, the triggers and consequent behaviour by keeping an emotions diary.

○ Develop their interpersonal and friendship skills by providing opportunities to model and practise positive social skills and social problem-solving.

○ Be aware of, and support, any additional learning needs.

○ Promote confidence and self-esteem by using personal strengths and interests to engage children in activities, and agree how best to praise and reward children. This could include keeping praise specific and in the here and now, and adopting a low-key approach.

'What strategies and approaches do you have in school to help children notice and manage their emotions, and what do you want to develop?'

5 Risk factors linked to significant life events

Many children will face difficult and traumatic life events, and although some children will be more resilient than others, difficult life events can be a trigger for mental health problems. We can't always predict how children will respond and cope with significant life events, but we do know that children are at greater risk of problems when these events occur alongside other stressful factors.

Significant life events that can be risk factors include:

- bereavement
- loss through parental separation or illness
- friendship difficulties
- transitions such as changing school, moving house or the birth of siblings
- exposure to natural disasters and war.

The following sections highlight how significant life events, such as transition and change, friendship difficulties and bullying, and bereavement and loss, can impact on mental health and behaviour. However the 'Five step framework' encourages us to be curious about all the risk factors that may be present.

Using the case studies

The purpose of the case studies is to highlight some of the risk factors that can impact on mental health and behaviour. However, it is important to remember that the presence of risk factors does not necessarily lead to mental health problems, but that awareness of risk factors and warning signs can help inform early identification and support. As such, the case studies are not intended to be used as a diagnostic tool, but to provide examples of using a five step framework when considering behavioural concerns.

The children in the case studies don't exist but reflect some of the typical concerns shared in consultations. Please note that the consultation questions were worked through over a series of sessions.

Bullying

Case study: Terri, Year 5

Consultation process overview

STEP 1. **What can we see?** The first step is to summarise the concerns about Terri's progress, starting with a description of her behaviour, and thinking about how often it occurs, how long it lasts and where it usually happens.

STEP 2. **What have we tried?** Reflecting on the strategies and interventions already tried in school, and their impact.

STEP 3. **What do we know?** Bringing together what we already know about Terri. In order to consider a wider perspective, this includes incorporating Terri's own views and the views of those who know her best, such as her family, as well as looking at information held in school.

STEP 4. **What is the mental health message?** Reflecting on what we understand about Terri's difficulties, thinking about risk factors and warning signs, to consider a link between mental health and behaviour. Can we identify or predict any emerging mental health problems?

STEP 5. **What would personalised planning look like for Terri?** Finally, in light of this understanding how can we best support her? How can we strengthen protective factors for mental health and implement targeted mental health support?

Step 1: What can we see?

Q What her teachers say. . .

Terri joined us midway through Year 4 after having previously attended several different schools because of family circumstances. When she arrived with us, we had very few records from her previous school or information about why she had moved around so frequently, so we had no idea what to expect. The short reports we did receive all said they had limited information to share because of the problems getting to know Terri, as she hadn't stayed in any one school for very long. However, one report mentioned domestic violence in the home and another said that Terri's behaviour could be moody and unsociable. Nevertheless, she settled in quite well and we had no real issues during the first half term. She established a group of friends in her class fairly quickly and was making small steps in academic progress, although she was working well below age expected levels. We thought this could be due to her unsettled education and the impact of changing schools so often and we hoped to see her make more progress once she had been with us for some time. However, although she is making slow, steady progress, teacher assessment suggests that she is still working significantly below expected levels.

Towards the end of Year 4, there were a few concerns from some of the other girls about Terri's bossiness – but no major issues. However in Year 5, we gradually learned about Terri's threatening and bullying behaviour towards some of the other girls. Apparently this had been going on for some time, but it was only when a parent came into school because of bruising to her daughter's upper arm, that we began to look more closely at this friendship group. Through a series of observations and interviews with some of the children, we learned that Terri had become increasingly vindictive and controlling in her comments. Terri is also very physical in her play – pushing and pulling the other girls in quite a rough way. Although these actions were usually targeted towards one particular girl with special needs, the rest of the group had felt sufficiently intimidated that they were unable to tell anyone about what they were witnessing.

Since confronting Terri about her behaviour she has become increasingly non-compliant and argumentative with staff. Most of the time she denies having done anything inappropriate and says that staff are 'picking on her' and 'out to get her'. A few times when we have been talking to her, she has zipped her coat over her head to blank us out.

We have reinforced a zero tolerance of any bullying behaviour in school, but Terri doesn't seem to understand or acknowledge that her behaviour is unacceptable. We have talked to Terri about the need to respect other people's personal space, and that it is inappropriate to use physical methods to direct others. She is supervised closely at break time and lunchtime but we can't be there all of the time. The other children are now more aware of the need to tell an adult about any bullying or intimidating behaviour, and they continue to report Terri's rough play, verbal threats and insults.

Step 2: What have we tried?

◌ What her teachers say. . .

We have firmly told Terri that her behaviour is unacceptable and that if it continues she will be at risk of exclusion. This doesn't seem to have any effect.

We have implemented a report card, which is signed by an adult at the end of each session, break time and lunchtime to monitor her behaviour. We have linked this to a series of rewards for positive reports and sanctions for negative reports. This had some initial short-term impact but doesn't seem to be an effective long-term strategy.

We have worked with the whole class to promote anti-bullying strategies and to encourage the children to report any negative behaviour, without specifically targeting Terri. Terri was part of this work and seemed oblivious to the fact that she was actually the perpetrator of much of this behaviour!

We have told Terri's mum about her behaviour but she became quite distressed and agitated, and said Terri wasn't like that at home and found it difficult to believe.

Terri works in a small group for literacy and numeracy and her work is highly differentiated.

Step 3: What do we know?

📄 Summary of key information from Terri's school file

- There is very limited information on file due to Terri's frequent change of school.
- She is currently working well below age expected levels and staff think this may be due to Terri's disrupted school experience so far. However, staff are now concerned about possible learning difficulties.

💬 What her parents say. . .

I am so upset about what the teacher said about Terri's behaviour. I find it hard to believe we are talking about the same girl – she is not like that at all at home. If anything, I would say she is timid and shy. They have asked me to go on a parenting course, but her behaviour isn't any trouble for me so I don't think I need it.

My new partner has two teenage girls who stay with us every weekend and Terri will barely look at them, let alone talk to them or give them cheek! She is very nervous and quiet around them, and seems to lack any confidence. I was hoping she would enjoy having stepsisters after all of the trouble we had with her dad. Unfortunately he was quite violent towards me so we had to move around a few times to try to make a fresh start. Now that he is out of the picture and we are settled I am really puzzled by these reports about Terri.

💬 What Terri says. . .

Terri put her head on the desk and was uncomfortable talking about her feelings, so her teacher used some pictures to explore Terri's views. She encouraged Terri to draw the girl she would 'most like to be' and the girl she would 'least like to be'. In this way, Terri was more able to share some of her views. Some of the comments Terri made while drawing are summarised below.

The girl I would most like to be is:

- Smart
- Clever
- Popular

- Happy
- Confident
- Friendly

The girl I would least like to be is:

- Stupid
- Lonely
- Invisible

Terri went on to say that she was afraid of her two stepsisters who called her horrible names, including: 'stupid', 'thick' and 'fat'.

Step 4: What is the mental health message?

Given what we now know about Terri, can we identify any emerging mental health challenges, or identify an increased vulnerability of developing mental health problems? What are the risk factors and warning signs?

Key points from the consultations

- Terri has changed schools several times due to family circumstances.
- There is a history of domestic violence.
- Her mother has now settled with a new partner and there is no contact with Terri's father.
- Terri can demonstrate threatening and abusive behaviour in school and particularly targets one other child.
- She shows limited awareness or understanding of her behaviour.
- Her mother reports that at home Terri's behaviour is timid, shy and unsure with her partner's children.
- Terri says that her stepsisters call her names and are unkind to her.
- Terri is making slow academic progress and working well below age expected levels. Her teachers are beginning to wonder if she could have learning difficulties.

Could her behaviour reflect any emerging mental health problems?

Emerging mental health problems – risk factors and warning signs

1. Aggressive and bullying behaviour

Terri is displaying aggressive and bullying behaviour towards her peers. When children engage in bullying behaviour it is important to explore the possible reasons for this, which could include their own mental health and emotional needs. There are several risk factors in Terri's life, and her behaviour may be a reaction to her own distress and unmet mental health and learning issues.

For instance, sometimes bullying behaviour can be a way of preventing isolation and gaining self-esteem. It is not unusual for children who bully others to be a victim of bullying themselves. We know that Terri has said that her stepsisters are unkind to her and call her names, and her mother says she is timid and shy at home.

2. Family history of domestic violence and disruption

There is limited information about Terri's family history, but we do know that she has moved house and changed school several times. We also know that there have been episodes of domestic violence in the family home, although we don't know the extent of this. A family history of domestic violence and disruption can be a risk factor for mental health problems. Studies suggest that domestic violence can be linked to emotional and behavioural problems, including anxiety, depression, poor school performance, low self-esteem, disobedience and physical health complaints (*The world report on violence and health*, Krug et al). We know that children who have witnessed domestic violence are more likely to become involved in a violent and abusive relationship themselves. Sometimes in these situations, children can copy the behaviour and strategies of their parents, or become 'desensitised' to aggression. Consequently some children may find it difficult to understand and form relationships.

We also know that domestic violence is very often associated with other risk factors within the family including poverty, substance abuse, parental mental health problems, and parenting style. Even if Terri has not directly witnessed abuse, it is highly likely that living with domestic violence will have had an impact on her early experiences, including her experience of early care and parenting, security and safety.

3. Transition and change

Terri has changed school and home several times. She started her current school midway through Year 4 when friendship groups are often already well-established. Although a part of life, transition and change can be risk factors for mental health problems, especially when they occur alongside other risk factors. Because of the number of transitions and amount of change in her life, Terri may not have had the opportunity to experience a sense of belonging and to develop positive social skills with her peers. We know that starting a new school part way through the school year can be particularly challenging and this may have contributed to her difficulties.

4. Learning needs

Terri may have unmet learning needs which will require further investigation. Difficulties with learning can be a risk factor for mental health challenges and can impact on social interaction and understanding. There has been limited information shared about Terri's learning due to a lack of record keeping and continuity in her education. It is possible that any learning needs have been missed and remain unidentified. If Terri has additional learning challenges these may be contributing to her behaviour in school.

Although children with additional needs are more at risk of being victims of bullying, they may also engage in bullying themselves as a means of self-preservation.

> *'Young people who were isolated, who were having mental health or emotional difficulties or who felt at risk of bullying themselves spoke of bullying others to enhance their social standing or to prevent that person from bullying them.' (Anti-bullying alliance)*

Conclusion

There are several risk factors for Terri that increase her vulnerability of developing mental health problems, and there are some signs to suggest that mental health challenges could underpin her current behaviour. Therefore staff should consider personalised approaches to support Terri that take these factors into account.

Step 5: What would personalised planning look like for Terri?

Whole school approaches and systems

A personalised approach would need to consider how whole school approaches and systems can support Terri, including:

- Clarifying proactive whole school strategies to promote anti-bullying and agree responses to episodes of bullying behaviour.
- Terri's ongoing assessment needs, including how staff will: monitor and review her mental health challenges; know when to refer on; clarify her learning needs, for example referring to an advisory teacher or educational psychologist.
- How the pastoral team can support Terri, and exploring the possibility of counselling support.

- Building in multi-agency review schedules to continue to share information with school staff and the family about her progress – this should also address her ongoing needs at home with her stepsisters, as well as at school.

Protective factors for good mental health and resilience

A personalised approach would promote protective factors for good mental health and resilience as well as supporting emerging mental health problems. (See Chapter 2, page 17) Protective factors for good mental health include:

- Being able to communicate with others and engage socially
- Having support for educational and learning needs
- Having a sense of belonging and good peer influences in school
- Feeling safe to raise and discuss problems.

Therefore a personalised approach for Terri would include strategies to investigate and support her learning needs and behaviour, as well as thinking about how to promote positive social skills and relationships, develop her emotional awareness and understanding, and social problem-solving skills.

Some specific strategies and approaches to support Terri's individual needs include:

1. Supporting positive peer relationships and social skills

This could be achieved by:

- Helping Terri to engage and interact with other children in a positive way. For example, think about how the PSHE curriculum promotes positive friendship skills to reduce bullying and conflict. What additional support does Terri need to develop positive relationships with others? What opportunities are there for peer support and peer mentoring, such as buddies and befrienders?

- Providing small group sessions where Terri can practise social and friendship skills and problem-solving, in an adult-led situation. Think about circle time activities and structured approaches such as circle of friends (see Chapter 4, page 74). Does Terri have opportunities to work with other children in a cooperative way to complete tasks? Use circle time, role play and drama to reinforce positive social and friendship skills, and to re-enact, reframe and understand situations that have occurred or may occur.

- Using restorative approaches to bullying incidents that focus on developing Terri's awareness of her behaviour, the school ethos, and the consequences of her behaviour on others.

2. Promoting her emotional awareness and understanding

This could be achieved by:

- Helping Terri to communicate positively during play and interactions by supporting her to understand and name her emotions – it will be important to help Terri develop a vocabulary for emotions so she is more confident in recognising her own emotions as well as those of others.
- Helping Terri to make links between her emotions and behaviour. For example, encourage Terri to identify situations where she feels certain emotions, and to manage her emotions in a positive way – work with her to find out what works best for her.
- Helping Terri to understand her inappropriate behaviour through activities that focus on empathy and social problem-solving. For example, help Terri to think about real-life situations by using pictures and drawings to explore problems. Help Terri to understand the impact of her behaviour on others.

3. Supporting her learning challenges and promoting her self-esteem and confidence

This could be achieved by:

- Gaining awareness of her strengths and interests and incorporating this information to develop her self-esteem.
- Ensuring that Terri's individual learning needs are identified and supported.
- Thinking about her need for predictability and security by planning carefully for transitions and change whenever possible.
- Promoting positive connections to school through encouraging Terri to take part in extracurricular activities, and exploring responsibilities and jobs Terri can be involved in.
- Providing opportunities for Terri to share information about her relationships and worries with her step sisters at home, through pastoral support or counselling.

At a glance...

Bullying

- There can be many reasons why children engage in bullying behaviour. When children bully others it is important to explore the possible reasons for this, which could include their own mental health and emotional needs.

- Sometimes bullying behaviour can be a way of preventing isolation and gaining self-esteem. It is not unusual for children who bully others to be a victim of bullying themselves.

- We know that children who have witnessed domestic violence are more likely to become involved in a violent and abusive relationship themselves. Sometimes in these situations, children can copy the behaviour and strategies of their parents, or become 'desensitised' to aggression.

- Be aware that support might be needed for the mental health and emotional well-being of both the child being bullied and the child displaying bullying behaviour.

- Support strategies for children who engage in bullying behaviour include:

  ○ Proactive whole school strategies to promote anti-bullying and having agreed responses to episodes of bullying behaviour.

  ○ Developing positive peer relationships and social skills by helping children to engage and interact with others in a positive way. Use circle time, role play and drama to reinforce positive social and friendship skills, and to re-enact, reframe and understand situations that have occurred or may occur.

  ○ Developing emotional awareness and understanding to help children understand how their behaviour impacts others, and to explore ways of recognising and managing their own emotions.

  ○ Using restorative approaches to bullying incidents that focus on developing individual awareness of their behaviour, the school ethos, and the consequences of their behaviour on others.

  ○ Ensuring the child's individual learning needs are identified and supported.

  ○ Using the child's strengths and interests to develop self-esteem and to engage in activities.

  ○ Working with the family to monitor and review behaviour and to consider the need for other support, including counselling.

'How does your school encourage peer support through, for example, peer mentoring schemes, anti-bullying ambassadors and buddy systems?'

Bereavement and loss

Case study: Saul, Year 3

Consultation process overview

STEP 1. **What can we see?** The first step is to summarise the concerns about Saul's progress, starting with a description of his behaviour, and thinking about how often it occurs, how long it lasts and where it usually happens.

STEP 2. **What have we tried?** Reflecting on the strategies and interventions already tried in school, and their impact.

STEP 3. **What do we know?** Bringing together what we already know about Saul. In order to consider a wider perspective, this includes incorporating Saul's own views and the views of those who know him best, such as his family, as well as looking at information held in school.

STEP 4. **What is the mental health message?** Reflecting on what we understand about Saul's difficulties, thinking about risk factors and warning signs, to consider a link between mental health and behaviour. Can we identify or predict any emerging mental health problems?

STEP 5. **What would personalised planning look like for Saul?** Finally, in light of this understanding how can we best support him? How can we strengthen protective factors for mental health and implement targeted mental health support?

Step 1: What can we see?

◯ What his teachers say…

Saul has always been a studious, hard-working little boy with lots of support from home. Sadly his father died suddenly in a road traffic accident almost a year ago, so understandably he needed a lot of support in the weeks and months following the bereavement. We thought he was coping as well as he could, given the situation, but over the past month or so his behaviour and attitude to school has changed dramatically. Some days he can be challenging, rude and aggressive to the adults in class, and at other times he seems totally switched off, lethargic and disengaged, unable to work or even pick up his pencil. Almost a year on we thought things would be settling down for Saul, but rather than things getting better with time, they actually seem to be getting much worse.

Although his grief is less visible in that he is rarely tearful now, his mood changes on a daily basis and we know this is having an impact on his progress and engagement, as well as on the rest of the class. Tears have transformed into anger, with regular outbursts of aggression. He has sworn at staff and become very distraught, often asking to go home. When we refuse to send him home, he shouts that he wants to be excluded. Sometimes he can't complete his work because of this behaviour, and he often seems either totally switched off, or extremely angry.

In some ways, Saul is more preoccupied with his father's death now than he was in the months after it happened. It is really difficult in class to know what to do. Saul often wants to turn all conversations and lessons round to talking about death and dying, and these emotions are 'catching'. Lots of children then want to talk about their losses, such as the death of grandparents or pets, and it seems as if this topic is taking over in the classroom.

The highly charged emotional atmosphere in class is having an impact on classroom teaching in general. We are worried that almost a year after his father's death, Saul's behaviour has declined and is having a massive impact on the classroom dynamics and atmosphere. Saul isn't making any progress and we feel a little out of our depth. Nearly a year after his father's death, we thought things would have been back on an even footing but instead they are getting worse.

Saul is sometimes late for school and on these days he can appear particularly tired, lethargic, and difficult to engage. His head will go down on the desk and he seems to have lost all motivation. This is very different to the Saul we knew a year ago who was a lively and willing participant in class. Before the bereavement he was one of the high achievers. Now he is just scraping through, working well below his own potential. We expected him to go through various stages of grief but we didn't expect this regression and total change in behaviour. It is such a sad situation.

We don't really know what is happening at home as we haven't had a great deal of contact with his mum over the past year. We don't want to bother her at this difficult time and we suspect she wants to keep her distance at the moment. She rarely comes into the playground at home time to chat with his teacher but instead waits for him outside the school gates. We feel as if she wants to avoid contact with us and we have to respect that. We wonder if Saul would benefit from counselling, but we are worried about burdening his mum with worries about his behaviour when she already has so much to cope with.

Step 2: What have we tried?

ℚ What his teachers say. . .

In the early weeks and months after the bereavement we allocated a teaching assistant (TA) to work alongside Saul. She was able to build a close relationship with him and respond to his distress in those difficult first weeks. Saul was also able to speak to the TA about his father, and together they made a memory book.

We were advised to keep some routine and consistency for him, so we tried to encourage him to get back to a normal school routine as soon as possible as we thought this would help, especially as his routine at home was likely to be very different.

Communication with Saul's mum isn't great, and we don't want to worry her even more. She comes in to school when we ask her to, but she doesn't seem fully engaged. The class teacher is reluctant to burden her with our concerns.

We have a reward system in place for Saul when he completes his work. This has had some intermittent success. At times we see flashes of the old Saul, but at other times he will say he doesn't care and everything is stupid.

Step 3: What do we know?

🗐 Summary of key information from Saul's school file

- There is limited information on school file as, prior to the bereavement, there were *no* concerns about Saul's behaviour and academic achievement.

- He was noted to be one of the high achievers in school and an engaged and motivated learner.

- He was previously achieving above age expected levels. His attainment levels have not progressed since his father's death and he is underachieving in school.

💬 What his mum says. . .

Saul's teacher has met with me to share some of the concerns about his behaviour in school. It has come as a bit of a shock to be honest, and I know I haven't been there for him as much as I should have. This past year has been a struggle. Some days I have simply been exhausted and haven't had the energy to leave the house or look after myself, let alone Saul. I know I have been living in a bit of a 'bubble', and perhaps this has made things even more difficult for him. Recently I have been talking to a counsellor, which has really helped me get things off my chest and to think about the future for the first time in ages. Now it is coming up to a year since Craig's death, I know it's time to start to move on.

I have had a lot of support from my own mother, Saul's gran, and recently I have had more good days than bad. I even went out with some friends again last week for the first time. Saul really didn't like that and refused to stay at his gran's house, which was strange because he usually really enjoys it there.

I suppose Saul has become quite controlling recently, and I know he worries about me a lot. Sometimes he will say he wants to stay at home with me rather than go to school. He will say he is ill, that there is something wrong with his head, or his stomach… he often complains about aches and pains. I believed him at first, but now I know it is an excuse because he doesn't want to go to school. It can be a struggle getting him out of the house in the morning, a real battle of wills, and sometimes I have to call his gran to come and drive him there because I don't have the energy.

I am worried that I haven't been able to support Saul properly. I still find it really hard to talk about his father with him, as it is all still so raw for both of us. I really don't want to open old wounds and make things even worse. I hope, in time, he will get back to the old Saul. He used to be sporty and loved being outdoors but all of that has changed now. I suppose he has become quite clingy. Now that I know how difficult he has been at school I am really worried about him.

♀ What Saul says. . .

The TA spent some time with Saul to understand his feelings about home and school. He was comfortable using a rating scale to indicate how he felt about different areas of his life.

On a scale of 1–10, where 10 is the most positive number, Saul rated the following;

School	1 2 ③ 4 5 6 7 8 9 10	He said he would rather be at home as school is 'boring'.
Lessons*	1 2 ③ 4 5 6 7 8 9 10	Similarly he said lessons were 'boring'.
***Art**	1 2 3 4 ⑤ 6 7 8 9 10	
Friends	1 2 ③ 4 5 6 7 8 9 10	He said that he had plenty of friends but that they sometimes get on his nerves, and sometimes they laugh and make nasty jokes about his dad when he falls out with them.
Home	1 2 3 4 5 6 ⑦ 8 9 10	He said he liked to be with his mum but doesn't like it when she goes out. He said he hates it when she leaves him with his gran because it makes him sick and poorly
Watching TV	1 2 3 4 5 6 7 ⑧ 9 10	
Playing on the computer	1 2 3 4 5 6 7 8 ⑨ 10	He said this is what he likes to do most of all.

Step 4: What is the mental health message?

Given what we now know about Saul, can we identify any emerging mental health challenges, or an increased vulnerability of developing mental health problems? What are the risk factors and warning signs?

Key points from the consultations

- Saul's father died suddenly almost a year ago.
- Saul's behaviour and attitude to school have changed recently.

- His behaviour is described as either challenging, rude and aggressive or switched off, lethargic and disengaged.
- He is no longer making academic progress, and his teacher thinks he is underachieving.
- School staff have had limited interaction with Saul's mother following the bereavement – staff have felt they need to respect her need for space and have feared upsetting her.
- The classroom atmosphere is described as 'highly charged' with a focus on death and dying, which is having an impact on classroom teaching in general.
- Saul no longer enjoys school and says that some children now laugh at him and make jokes about his father.
- His mother acknowledges she has been unable to be there for him emotionally, but that she is now feeling more resilient.

Could his behaviour reflect emerging mental health problems?

Emerging mental health problems – risk factors and warning signs

1. Significant traumatic life event

Saul has experienced a significant traumatic life event with the death of his father. Sadly, many children will experience the death of a close family member or friend. Many of these children will be able to adapt to their loss without experiencing any mental health problems or need for additional support. Nevertheless their reactions to the bereavement may be apparent for some time following the loss. Typical reactions can involve a wide range of emotions and behaviours, including: high levels of distress, guilt or occupation with the loss; anxiety; withdrawal; panic; loss of concentration; ongoing distress and family problems. It is important to note that children will respond to bereavement in different ways. The process of grief can differ in how it looks and how long it lasts – there is no 'right' or 'wrong' way to grieve.

> *'Up to 70% of schools have a bereaved pupil on their roll at any given time. One study found that 92% of young people will experience a significant bereavement before the age of 16 years. (Child bereavement UK)*

Many children will adapt well to bereavement and loss, but there is some evidence to suggest that children who are parentally bereaved have an increased risk of mental health issues, lower academic attainment, lower self-esteem and increased feelings of helplessness. Studies suggest that even when children's initial responses to grief lessen over time, there may still be long lasting effects on mental health and resilience, with links between parental bereavement and longer-term depressive symptoms.

Some children may be at increased risk of mental health problems because of other pressures resulting from the bereavement, such as financial or housing difficulties, or physical or mental health issues within the family. Other children may have individual factors that could increase their vulnerability, such as their temperament, personality or learning needs. A child's ability to manage their grief may be affected by the interplay of these additional stressful events and individual factors, therefore it is important that support focuses on minimising additional stressors whenever possible, while at the same time building the child's inner and external resources for coping and problem-solving.

Akerman and Statham's report, *Bereavement in childhood: the impact on psychological and educational outcomes and the effectiveness of support services* recommends a range of support for bereaved children. It suggests that this should include individual strategies tailored to the personal needs of the child, as well as whole school approaches, such as 'programmes to strengthen all children's resilience, including elements relating to their capacity to respond to their own or their peers' experiences of death, or to educate teachers in the ways that children grieve.'

2. Change in behaviour

Saul's change in behaviour could be a sign that he is not coping with the bereavement. Signs that a child is not coping can include: increased anxiety, low mood and depressive symptoms, fears, angry outbursts, and regression of skills. Sometimes 'acting out' behaviour can reflect internal feelings of anger, terror, frustration and helplessness. It is possible that Saul's 'acting out' behaviour is a reflection of his own insecurity and feelings of helplessness, and may be his way of imposing his own control on the situation. Saul may be unable to share his grief and worries openly, and so may be demonstrating his frustrations through his behaviour.

Sometimes Saul's behaviour is described as lethargic and unmotivated. This 'acting in' behaviour could be a sign that Saul is feeling anxious. He will ask to go home or to be excluded, and it may even be possible that he has some worries about his mother and wants to be close to her. His mother tells us that Saul often complains about feeling physically unwell. Although it is common for children to display reactions for some time after a bereavement, it is the increasing intensity of Saul's behaviour which is a trigger for concern. His behaviour is now having a significant impact on his progress in school as well as the wider class group.

3. Social isolation

Saul's social support networks appear limited. His mother acknowledges that she hasn't been emotionally available for Saul because of her own grief. It is possible that Saul has felt isolated, alone and abandoned not only by the death of his father, but also by the emotional unavailability of his mother. Saul is fairly negative in his opinions of school and his friendships, despite teacher reports that he used to be an enthusiastic, outgoing individual. He says that some of his friends have laughed about his father's death. Social networks and friendships are a very important protective factor following a bereavement, but sometimes the bereavement itself can influence these. Children who have been bereaved can sometimes be identified as 'different' and become the target of bullying and teasing.

Conclusion

We recognise that Saul's behaviour could reflect mental health challenges – there are several risk factors that increase his vulnerability, and signs suggest that emerging mental health challenges could underpin his current behaviour. Therefore staff should consider personalised approaches to support Saul that take these factors into account.

Step 5: What would personalised planning look like for Saul?

Whole school approaches and systems

A personalised approach would need to consider whole school approaches and systems to support Saul, including:

- How the pastoral support system can support Saul, and exploring the need for counselling support.

- Ensuring staff have a good understanding of grief and don't assume that the process of grief will pass through stages in an orderly or predictable way – think about the ongoing training and support needs.

- Having an agreed school policy for supporting bereaved children which is available for all staff in school – this would include information about how to support bereaved children, as well as the process of grief and self-care for staff.

- Planning how the school will engage with Saul's mother to continue to share information about his progress and ongoing needs, to support her management of Saul, and to build in regular reviews.

- Thinking about Saul's ongoing assessment needs and how staff will monitor and measure his mental health challenges and know when to refer on if necessary.

Protective factors for good mental health and resilience

A personalised approach would promote protective factors for good mental health and resilience, as well as supporting emerging mental health problems. (See Chapter 2, page 17) Some of the protective factors that can support bereaved children include:

- Being able to experience achievement and promote self-esteem. According to a study by Brewer and Sparkes, some parentally bereaved children have said that having an area of competence was one of the factors that helped them get through their grief – this included extra-curricular activities as well as academic achievements.

- Having healthy beliefs about control and a range of coping strategies to identify and manage emotions. This incudes recognising those situations in which individuals can have an impact, and identifying helpful ways to manage emotional responses.

- Having a positive relationship with the surviving parent to help the child adjust to the bereavement and finding ways to keep the memory of their deceased parent alive.

- Being able to express emotion – it is important that children do not feel inhibited should they need to express and explore their feelings.

Some specific strategies and approaches to support Saul's individual needs in school would focus on creating a safe space for him to share his emotions, as well as building his coping skills, self-esteem, sense of self efficacy and social supports. This could include:

1. Enabling Saul to identify, express and manage his emotions in school with a counsellor or a key person on a regular basis

This could be achieved by:

- Helping him understand his emotions, worries and anxieties and how best to manage them positively. For example, encouraging Saul to talk about his feelings and grief may offer him some reassurance, as well as giving him an insight into any emerging or changing emotions. This could help reduce any further anxieties of loss and separation.

- Developing his coping strategies and sense of self-efficacy. To reduce Saul's feelings of helplessness, staff should support Saul to set his own personal goals and targets, and give him positive and constructive feedback about his coping strategies. This will help to promote his resilience and sense that he will be able to manage future difficulties and challenges.

- Providing him with information on a needs-led basis about bereavement and grief and what it means to him, and opportunities for him to talk about and remember his father.

2. Helping him to enjoy and achieve his potential in class by offering specific strategies to regulate his emotions

These should be discussed and developed with Saul but could include:

- The use of signals such as happy or sad faces, or red or green cards that can be placed on the table to signal how he feels that day so the teacher can respond accordingly.

- Time out cards if he needs some personal space to manage his emotions.

- Encouraging Saul to find ways of self-soothing in class when he feels anxious, upset or angry. This could include discrete strategies such as the use of pocket comforters, for example a small piece of fabric or pebble which can be carried in his pocket, as well as having a box of calming activities available, such as colouring tasks, listening to music or relaxation tapes.

3. Supporting his connection to school, his sense of self-esteem and achievement

This could be achieved by:

- Helping Saul to feel a sense of belonging and connectedness in school. As he has identified some emerging concerns about his friendships and increased negativity about school, think about introducing some strategies to promote opportunities to develop social interactions and friendships.

- Introducing whole class discussions to plan how children can support each other better. For example, think about buddying approaches and introduce whole class rewards for targeted behaviour. Strategies such as 'marbles in the jar' (see Chapter 3, page 61) can foster a sense of camaraderie, well-being and support.

- Encouraging Saul to take on areas of special responsibility and use his strengths and interests to re-engage him in school.

4. Supporting the needs of the whole class in order to encourage social support and empathy

This could be achieved by:

- Thinking about how circle time activities and PSHE lessons can give space to safely address issues of grief and loss.

- Supporting children to name and manage their difficult emotions through relaxation, breathing exercises and mindfulness based activities, which can be used throughout the day when staff feel that emotions are 'catching' and taking over.

- Considering how Saul's distress and grief may bring about some of his classmates' fears and anxieties, or memories of their own losses. Discuss how grief can affect us all in different ways to help normalise and accept emotions.

At a glance...

Bereavement and loss

- **Grief can be a coping response to any loss, and loss can be experienced in several different situations, including: loss experienced through bereavement, relationship break ups, loss of friendships, illness, and change of home or school.**

- Up to 70% of schools have a bereaved pupil on their role at any given time (Child Bereavement UK). Many of these children will be able to adapt to their loss without experiencing any mental health problems or need for additional support.

- Although there can be different stages to grief, these stages are not always linear and clear.

- Reactions to bereavement may be apparent for some time after the loss. Reactions are likely to vary but can include: high levels of distress, guilt or occupation with the loss, anxiety, withdrawal, panic, loss of concentration and ongoing distress and family problems.

- Bereavement of a close family member or friend can place children at greater risk of mental health issues. Risks are increased when there are additional stressful events (such as housing or financial issues or parental mental health problems) and can also be affected by risk factors in the child such as personality, temperament, learning needs and problem-solving ability.

- Support for bereaved children should consider strategies tailored to the individual needs of the bereaved child, while also providing whole school approaches to develop understanding and resilience.

- When supporting children who have faced significant bereavement or loss, it is important to:

   ◦ Remember that many children will adapt to their loss without experiencing any mental health problems or need for additional support.

   ◦ Understand that some children may be at greater risk of developing mental health problems – this includes children who are parentally bereaved.

   ◦ Be vigilant for signs that a child may not be coping. Risk factors include children who face additional stressful situations and have limited coping strategies or additional difficulties. Signs that a child may not be coping may differ but will have a significant impact on functioning in school and at home. Signs can include: severe loss of interest in activities, a change in their usual eating or sleeping patterns, school refusal, significant change in their ability to learn and achieve, an overwhelming preoccupation with death and dying.

   ◦ Create a safe space for the child to talk about their loss.

   ◦ Help the child to identify and understand their emotions and explore positive coping strategies.

   ◦ Promote the child's sense of self-efficacy by involving him or her in problem-solving and goal setting.

- Build coping skills, self-esteem and social supports. Ensure the child feels connected to school by building on strengths and interests so they can experience a sense of achievement. Strengthen social networks and friendship groups in school.

- Think about how school can support and maintain a relationship with the family so that they in turn, can support their child.

 'Do you have clear and agreed approaches to supporting bereaved pupils in your school, which includes information about the process of grief and self-care for staff?'

Transition and change
Case study: Stacie, Year 6

Consultation process overview

STEP 1. **What can we see?** The first step is to summarise the concerns about Stacie's progress, starting with a description of her behaviour, and thinking about how often it occurs, how long it lasts and where it usually happens.

STEP 2. **What have we tried?** Reflecting on the strategies and interventions already tried in school, and their impact.

STEP 3. **What do we know?** Bringing together what we already know about Stacie. In order to consider a wider perspective, this includes incorporating Stacie's own views and the views of those who know her best, such as her family, as well as looking at information held in school.

STEP 4. **What is the mental health message?** Reflecting on what we understand about Stacie's difficulties, thinking about risk factors and warning signs, to consider a link between mental health and behaviour. Can we identify or predict any emerging mental health problems?

STEP 5. **What would personalised planning look like for Stacie?** Finally, in light of this understanding how can we best support her? How can we strengthen protective factors for mental health and implement targeted mental health support?

Step 1: What can we see?

◯ What her teachers say...

Stacie has always been a high-achieving, sociable child who is eager to succeed and please. This term, however, we have seen a worrying change in her behaviour. If you didn't know her, you probably wouldn't think there was anything to be concerned about. On the surface she appears to be a quiet member of the class who goes with the flow, but we have noticed that she is no longer particularly engaged with her work or the other children, and is often distracted and subdued. This is so unlike her. When we first noticed this change, we thought it might be her hormones kicking in early, so we weren't that concerned. However, as the weeks have gone on, we have noticed that she often appears switched off, moody and negative.

Stacie has never had any behaviour issues in school and she is still generally well-behaved and compliant. On the face of it she seems to be working steadily and always finishes her tasks, but we have noticed that her work output is very much reduced and she lacks the care and effort she once had. Although we have had no major behavioural incidents, we have noticed that Stacie has occasionally been snappy and offhand to some adults in school. An example of this was when the head of Year 7 carried out a transition visit to the class. Stacie was quite rude and muttered under her breath throughout most of his talk. When we asked her about this she said she didn't want to go to the secondary school, that she had heard bad things about it, and she knew it would be 'rubbish'. She is very negative about lots of things now and this is casting a different atmosphere within the class. Her comments about the secondary school actually increased some of the other children's anxieties.

Stacie wants to stay in at break time and usually asks to play on the computer. She says her friends are picking on her, but she is very vague and we can't get to the bottom of this. Her friends appear puzzled by these accusations. We have asked some of the girls to make sure they include her and ask her to play, but Stacie is such hard work at the moment that I know they are finding this difficult.

In class, she seems to have developed a habit of whispering under her breath as she is working, which is further alienating her from the other children. We don't know what she is saying, and when we ask her to be quiet this seems to upset and agitate her, so we are trying to ignore it whenever we can.

Although Stacie isn't a problem for us in terms of behaviour management, we are worried about this change in her behaviour. We can't identify anything out of the ordinary that has happened to cause this. Although Stacie's mum and dad are divorced, this happened when she was very small and it all seems very amicable. Her mother and her father come to meetings in school together and still work together in Stacie's interests. Her mum has just had a baby with her second husband, Stacie's stepdad, who is also very much involved and supportive of Stacie.

Step 2: What have we tried?

○ What her teachers say. . .

We have tried talking to Stacie about anything that might be bothering her, and have pointed out the change in her behaviour, but when we did, Stacie became even more upset and so we didn't force the issue as we didn't want to make things worse for her.

We have been using positive rewards to encourage Stacie to do her very best work, but these no longer seem to motivate her. We have also encouraged some of the other children to buddy up with her at break time, but sometimes Stacie will say she wants to be inside on her own. We are ignoring some aspects of her behaviour such as the whispering and trying to downplay her negative comments.

We have spoken to her mother. She has just had a new baby and she has also noticed a change in Stacie's behaviour.

Step 3: What do we know?

📖 Summary of key information from Stacie's school file

- There is no information of note on Stacie's school file. She has always achieved above average expectations and there have been no previous behaviour concerns. Until recently she has been an engaged and sociable member of the class.

ᗧ What her parents say...

We are all very worried about Stacie. She seems down in the dumps at the moment and she cries very easily. When I try to talk to her about it she can be quite snappy with me. I've heard her being a bit snappy with her friends too, and I think they find this hard to understand. She used to be so enthusiastic about things, her dancing, netball, gym club... but now she says she is too tired, or that she is bored with these things. It's true that she has much less energy, so perhaps she really is too tired.

I took her to the doctors recently as she is often complaining about tiredness and headaches and I wondered if this could be hormonal. However he said he didn't think so and asked if there was anything she might be worried about in school that could be bringing these headaches on.

Stacie won't really talk about school but a couple of times she has said that some of the girls have been unkind to her. She says they talk about her behind her back and have told her she will be bullied at big school because she has red hair. It's nothing really serious, just the kind of silly things that girls of this age sometimes say to each other. I wonder if the move to secondary school is bothering her though.

Stacie has a new baby brother. He is almost three months old now and she hasn't been as involved with him as I imagined she would be. She seemed excited when I was pregnant and I thought she would have enjoyed bathing him and feeding him, but since his birth she's preoccupied and distant. We have just found out that her dad's new partner is also pregnant and Stacie has been very dismissive about this.

Recently she has started to do something a little strange. She has got into a habit of counting under her breath for no reason. I am a little worried about this, as it seems such an odd thing to do. When I asked her about it she became embarrassed and told me to leave her alone.

ᗧ What Stacie says...

Stacie worked with her class teacher to think about things she enjoys at home and at school and why she enjoys them, as well as the things she doesn't enjoy. Because she can be reluctant to share her views, the class teacher used some 'sentence starters' to help structure the conversations with Stacie, and to reduce her anxiety.

In school I like it when. . .

- I play netball
- I can play on the computer.
- I get things right.

In school I don't like it when. . .

- We have to do tests, especially practice tests for SATs.
- I have headaches and I can't concentrate.

At home I like it when. . .

- I watch TV, especially in my room
- I do my nails with my mum
- I can have my own bedroom.

At home, I don't like it when. . .

- I have to share my room with the baby because he cries at night and wakes me up. He is so noisy! I also don't like it when he has smelly nappies!

I like these things because. . .

- I am good at them, especially playing goal attack in netball. I like to score goals. When I am playing netball or computer games it is good fun as it takes all my concentration and I am not thinking of anything else.
- I like getting things right in school because I like to do well.

I don't like these things because. . .

- Tests make me feel really worried about doing well. I am worried about which class I will be in when I get to secondary school if I don't do well in my tests. This makes me feel sick and panicky. Sometimes my headaches get worse when there is a test.

I like doing these things because. . .

- They are fun.
- I like spending time with my mum.
- I like peace and quiet.

I don't like to think about. . .

- Leaving my school and going to big school. I am kind of looking forward to going to big school but also kind of scared as well. I am really worried about being in a class with none of my friends, and how I will make new friends. Some people say I will be bullied because I have red hair, but my mum won't let me dye it.

Step 4: What is the mental health message?

Given what we now know about Stacie, can we identify any emerging mental health challenges, or an increased vulnerability of developing mental health problems? What are the risk factors and warning signs?

Key points from the consultations

- Stacie's behaviour has changed recently.
- She is negative and disengaged and described as 'moody'.
- Although she continues to work steadily and always finishes her classroom tasks, her work output is reduced and she lacks the care and effort she once displayed.
- She is snappy and offhand with adults and her peers.
- She says her friends 'pick on' her.
- She is negative about her impending transition to secondary school.
- She is worried about losing her current friends and making new friends.
- She is worried about 'doing well' in the Year 6 tests.
- She whispers and counts under her breath in a repetitive way.
- Her mother has recently had a baby with Stacie's stepdad. Stacie shows limited interest in her new baby brother.
- Her father's partner is pregnant with their first child.

Could her behaviour reflect any emerging mental health problems?

Emerging mental health problems – risk factors and warning signs

1. Life events

Although the adults in Stacie's life can't pinpoint anything significant that has happened recently to cause this change in behaviour, there are several life events that involve change, uncertainty and an element of loss.

Transition to secondary school is a life event that can be a risk factor for emerging mental health problems. Some children will struggle with transition to secondary school, and this is more likely to happen if there are other risk factors present, which increases vulnerability. In Stacie's case, it is likely that the other changes and events in her life, as well as the impending transition, make her more vulnerable. Stacie's mother has recently had a baby and her father's partner is also pregnant. Stacie has referred to the pressure she feels under because of the impending SATs tests and worries about 'doing well'.

How we manage to cope with change and uncertainty often depends on our mental health, and although many children will cope with life changes, they will differ in their ability to manage and accept change. Individual characteristics such as personality and temperament, physical health and the other life events that might be occurring at the same time, can all affect children's mental health and resilience. Some children may therefore be more vulnerable and need support in order to minimise the risk of mental health problems. The multiple risk factors for Stacie, alongside the change in her behaviour, suggest that she has some emerging mental health needs.

2. Change in behaviour

Stacie's change in behaviour may be a sign of an emerging mental health problem. She is less motivated in school and there are several comments from adults about her low mood and negativity. This change in behaviour is having an impact on her schoolwork and on her friendships and is evident at home and at school. Stacie is withdrawing from her friends, has complained of feeling physically unwell, and lacks motivation for schoolwork. The adults who know her well, say this is unusual for Stacie. She has also developed a habit of counting under her breath and says she is worried about her Year 6 tests and the move to secondary school. It is possible that Stacie's change in behaviour is linked to emerging emotional problems of low mood and/or anxiety.

Low mood and anxiety

'Feeling sad is a normal reaction to experiences that are stressful or upsetting. However, when these feelings go on and on, take over your usual self and interfere with your whole life, it can become an illness. This illness is called "depression".' (Royal College of Psychiatrists)

Although a diagnosis of depression is less common in young children, it is important to be aware of the risk factors and signs that can signal when a child is at greater risk. Low mood can be displayed by a change in behaviour, including:

- A change in appetite, sleep or activity and concentration levels.
- Children may appear tearful, irritable, angry, tired or lethargic, or their mood may change rapidly.
- They might stop doing the things they once enjoyed and avoid social interactions.

  Be extra vigilant for a change in behaviour that is long lasting and for any signs of self-harm.

Stacie is worried and anxious about several different things in her life. Anxiety is one of the most common causes of distress in children and young people. Anxiety can run in families but things like physical illness, changes or unrest in the family, friendship difficulties and fear of bullying, are all common causes of anxiety in children. When several of these things happen at the same time this increases the risk of anxiety.

Anxiety can be displayed by a change in behaviour. Physical changes such as feeling breathless, tense, tearful or having sleeping problems can be common. Many children might say they feel physically unwell, and complain of sickness, tiredness or headaches.

Repetitive behaviour

Stacie has also developed a habit of counting under her breath in a repetitive way. Although Stacie doesn't want to discuss this with her mother, it is important that she is encouraged to find someone she can talk to safely so we can better understand this change in her behaviour. It may be that Stacie's repetitive counting is an obsessive habit, which could be a response to anxiety. Many of us will have intrusive thoughts from time to time, particularly in response to stress and worry. Sometimes these thoughts might make us do things over again, or feel compelled to do things in exactly the same way. Stacie may need support to recognise and address the worries that may be driving the behaviour and to find other ways to manage her anxiety. Although Stacie's counting does not seem to be significantly affecting her daily life, it is important that we find out more about this so that we can help her to understand and manage any anxiety, to minimise the risk of such behaviours and habits taking hold.

Conclusion

We recognise that Stacie's behaviour could reflect mental health challenges – there are several risk factors that increase her vulnerability, and there are some signs to suggest that emerging mental health challenges, linked to emotional difficulties such as anxiety and low mood, could underpin her current behaviour. Therefore staff should consider personalised approaches to support Stacie that take these factors into account.

Step 5: What would personalised planning look like for Stacie?

Whole school approaches and systems

A personalised approach would need to consider whole school approaches and systems to support Stacie, including:

- How staff will monitor and measure Stacie's mental health challenges and know when to refer on to other services – this includes finding out more about Stacie's behaviour and current coping strategies, to understand how best to support her.

- How pastoral support can help Stacie explore and manage her low mood and possible anxiety, for example through accessing counselling support.
- Building in review schedules to continue to share information with school staff and family about her progress, ongoing needs and how she can be supported at home and at school.
- Whole school approaches to supporting children through transition and exam stress, and how to identify and provide more targeted support for those who may be especially vulnerable.

Protective factors for good mental health and resilience

As well as supporting emerging mental heath needs, a personalised approach would build on protective factors for good mental health and resilience (see Chapter 2, page 17). Protective factors for good mental health include:

- Being able to identify your own and others' emotions
- Having opportunities to feel safe to discuss problems and to explore a range of solutions
- Maintaining good relationships and peer influences
- Promoting a sense of belonging in school and supporting children to understand that their views are important, heard and can make a difference. This can support the development of an internal sense of control. When children have an internal sense of control they are more likely to believe that they can make choices and are responsible for their own actions. This in turn, can support their decision-making and resilience when faced with future challenges.

Protective factors for Stacie would include thinking about how to prevent her social isolation, strengthen feelings of involvement and connection in school, as well as helping her to recognise and manage low mood, stress and anxiety. For Stacie, whole class sessions around transition and practical coping strategies for exams could help her develop a sense of control over some of the potentially stressful situations. Universal approaches, for example through PSHE delivery, can support all children to understand and manage their feelings and to practise positive coping strategies such as social problem-solving, and how to self-regulate or self-calm through relaxation or mindfulness based activities.

Some specific strategies and approaches to support Stacie's individual needs include:

1. Helping Stacie to identify, understand and manage her emotions, particularly in relation to low mood, anxiety and stress

This could be achieved by:

- Developing a trusting relationship with an adult in school, such as a key person or counsellor, so that Stacie can feel safe to share and explore her feelings.

- Supporting her to develop greater awareness of her emotions. For example, encourage her to identify the physical signs in her body when she feels different emotions, and to understand her own personal triggers.

- Helping Stacie to understand and identify her thoughts, and to recognise that some feelings of worry, stress and anxiety may be linked to her thoughts about situations. Draw attention to any unhelpful or unrealistic thoughts, such as predicting what is going to happen, looking though a 'negative lens' and discounting the positive, and 'mind reading' what others are thinking. Let Stacie know that these thinking errors can take over in times of stress. (See 'Common thinking errors' below.)

- Encouraging Stacie to monitor her worry and anxiety by keeping a diary of her personal triggers and responses (see Chapter 4, page 65). For example, encourage her to record: the things she is worried about, where she notices the worry in her body, the thoughts connected to the worry, and how this affects her behaviour.

Common thinking errors

How we think about things often impacts on how we feel and behave. Sometimes our thoughts can be helpful and at other times unhelpful. We can all slip into unhelpful ways of thinking from time to time. Occasionally we might get into a habit of thinking unhelpful thoughts. These unhelpful thoughts are sometimes called 'thinking errors'.

Some common thinking errors

- **Looking through a negative lens** – only focusing on the negatives. For example, you might have had a really good day in school, but at lunchtime you have to have mashed potato because there are no chips left. Later that evening when asked if you have had a good day, you say 'No, because I had to have mashed potato for lunch'.

- **Turning your back on the positive** – for example, you might get eight out of ten in a spelling test but dismiss the eight correct spellings, and only remember the two mistakes you made.

- **Black and white thinking** – sometimes known as 'all or nothing' thinking. Things are either fantastic or terrible, nothing in-between. Words like 'never', and 'always' are often found in black and white thinking. For example, 'I never get anything right'.

- **Mind reading** – assuming you know exactly what other people are thinking. For example, you walk past a group of people who are laughing, and you immediately think, 'They are laughing at me'.

Help children to notice and understand their thinking errors so that they can change them into more helpful thoughts. Encourage children to test their thoughts by asking, 'Is that thought helpful or unhelpful? Is that thought a fact and true? What is the evidence for that thought? Could that thought be a thinking error?'

2. Supporting Stacie to develop a range of problem-solving and coping skills

This could be achieved by:

- Using role play and story to work through challenging situations, discussing what she was thinking during these situations and exploring alternative problem-solving options by asking, 'Was that thought true or false? How did we know? What was the proof for that thought?' etc. Explore together some alternative ways of thinking about the situations.

- Supporting Stacie to understand more about common thinking errors and to challenge her own thinking errors. For example, does she 'mind read' as if she knows what the other person is thinking, or does she resort to 'catastrophising' or focusing on the worst thing that can possibly happen? Be curious and explore different thinking errors and ways of challenging them.

- Explore self-regulating and calming activities such as relaxation, breathing exercises or listening to music. Model positive stress reducing activities yourself. Find out the things that Stacie enjoys doing and encourage her to do these things more often.

- Create a safe place to go to in school when her stress levels are high, where she can practise some of her self-regulating activities.

3. Supporting transition planning

This could be achieved by:

- Thinking about the practical information that can help Stacie prepare for the transition. What does she need to know about her new school?

- Arranging extra visits to the school to help Stacie become familiar with the new environment.

- Supporting opportunities to attend extracurricular activities and clubs taking place at the school over the summer break.

- Liaising with key staff in her new school to share information about Stacie's individual needs and working with Stacie to write a pupil passport or profile to capture the information that she thinks staff need to know about her. Think about the things that are important to Stacie and how she thinks others can support her best.

4. Helping to reduce the impact of exam stress

This could be achieved by:

- Offering practical support, such as teaching Stacie how to plan ahead for the tests, using a homework/test timetable, and making sure she plans time to relax and do the things she enjoys.

- Helping her to prepare for the day of the tests by having a good breakfast, knowing where the test will be held, and helping her to make sure she has all of her equipment.

- Discussing practical exam techniques such as answering the questions she finds easiest first then going back to the other ones.

- Talking about the range of emotions she might feel on the day, and practising how to manage them. Explore self-calming activities such as focusing her attention on her breathing or on an object in the room.

At a glance. . .

Transition and change

- There are several life events that can involve change, uncertainty and an element of loss. Our ability to cope with these events often depends on our mental health.

- Although many children will cope with common life events and change, some children will be more vulnerable. Individual characteristics such as personality and temperament, physical health and the other things that might be going on in their lives at the same time, can all affect their ability to cope with transition and change. Children who are already exposed to several risk factors are more likely to experience greater difficulties.

- Transition to secondary school can be a risk factor for emerging mental health problems. Some children will struggle with transition to secondary school, and this is more likely to happen if there are other risk factors present, which increase vulnerability.

- A change in behaviour may be one of the first signs that a child is not coping with change. These behaviour changes may be linked to stress, anxiety or low mood.

- Feeling low or sad is something that we will all feel from time to time, especially in response to life events. When these feelings are long lasting and affect the person's life then they can become an illness like depression. It is important to be aware of the risk factors and signs that can signal a child is at greater risk in order to provide early support.

- Anxiety is one of the most common causes of distress in children and young people. Physical changes such as feeling breathless, tense, tearful or having sleeping problems can be common. Many children might say they feel physically unwell, and complain of sickness, tiredness or headaches.

- When supporting children who display anxiety/low mood, think about:

  - Helping them to identify, understand and manage their emotions. For example, encourage children to talk about their emotions in a trusting relationship with a key worker or counsellor. Help them to keep an 'emotions and triggers diary' (see page 95) to monitor and track their emotions.

  - Helping them to develop a range of problem-solving and coping skills. For example, talk through difficult situations by identifying the thoughts that underpin the emotions. Help them to understand and challenge some of the common thinking errors. Explore self-regulating and calming activities and create a safe place to self-calm in school when stress levels are high.

  - Preparing them for significant events such as transition and exams. For example, help children to prepare for events practically and look out for those who may be more vulnerable and need extra support.

 'How do you identify and support children who may find it more difficult to cope with change and transition?'

In conclusion

Making mental health matter for everyone

Understanding that behaviour conveys a message, and that the message may be about an unmet mental health need, is a step towards early identification and prevention. When we can confidently identify those children who are at risk and showing signs of emerging difficulties, the next step is to offer targeted early support.

The case studies have highlighted some of the risk factors, warning signs and behaviour when that unmet need is related to mental health issues, and have provided some ideas for personalised interventions. In identifying difficulties and providing timely and appropriate support, we hope to prevent emerging mental health problems from taking hold and escalating into more serious difficulties and disorders.

But prevention doesn't start with the identification of emerging problems, it needs to start much earlier than that...

We know that many adult mental health problems begin in childhood and that one in four of us will have some kind of mental health problem in the course of a year. For fewer of us to experience mental health problems in the first place, we need to become more mental health aware.

And this begins by talking about it.

When we stop the stigma around mental health – by talking about it, recognising it and learning how to look after it – then many children will be less likely to turn to unhealthy coping strategies, and display mental distress through their behaviour. Early intervention and prevention of mental health problems in school begins by promoting positive mental health and emotional well-being for everyone – adults as well as children. Everyone in the school environment can benefit from a culture that values the maintenance of positive mental health:

- Staff benefit from an ethos that encourages them to notice and care for their own mental health needs, particularly with regard to stress, in a non-stigmatising way.
- Children benefit from being taught to understand and manage their mental health – to become familiar with what is going on in their minds, how this links to what they feel and do, and what they can do to keep emotionally healthy.

All children need to know that feeling a range of fluctuating emotions is entirely normal, and that sometimes those emotions may be uncomfortable or difficult. Understanding the unhelpful thoughts that underpin emotions, and noticing and managing those thoughts before they take hold, is a vital skill for everyone, and not just those with mental health problems. And everyone, children and adults alike, benefit from supportive environments and relationships, so they can practise positive coping strategies, and develop the inner strengths and beliefs to face future challenges.

⌕ Looking through a mental health lens. . .

Make mental health matter in your school by regularly reflecting on the mental health needs of your children, staff, parents and community. Share what is going well and what needs some attention. Try using the following reflection points to start staff discussions and identify mental health priorities that matter in your school.

Reflection points for *universal* mental health matters

1. How does your school currently raise awareness of mental health and well-being?

- What does mental health mean to your school community? *Spend some time discussing the term mental health so you can come to a joint definition and shared understanding.*

- Are mental health matters openly discussed in your school, positives as well as negatives? *A shared narrative can help support a school culture where positive mental health and well-being is valued and mental health issues are acknowledged and kept alive.*

- Do staff talk openly to all children, and each other, about mental health in the same way they would physical health? *Do opportunities to talk about mental health permeate throughout the school day as well as through curriculum delivery, such as mental health focused PSHE lessons?*

- How do staff involve parents and children in mental health matters? *Think about opportunities for peer support, and how you can ensure parents and children have a voice and are heard.*

- What staff training and development opportunities are needed around positive mental health and well-being?

2. How is mental health care promoted for everyone?

- How does your school support the mental health of staff? *Remember the oxygen mask principle: adults need to put on their mask first!*

  - Working in schools can be stressful, how are staff encouraged to be aware of, and care for, their own mental health?

  - What opportunities do members of staff have to talk about and manage their own mental health, especially related to stress and anxiety?

  - Think about opportunities for peer support, time for reflection, whole staff development in areas of relaxation and mindfulness, physical activities and exercise, and social support.

  - How is staff well-being monitored and are there clear systems so staff can safely ask for help if it is needed?

- What is in place to teach all children how to look after their mental health?

  - Is mental health care addressed throughout the ethos of the school, as well as in PSHE lessons?

  - Are children explicitly taught how to look after their minds as well as their bodies? Does this include how to notice, name and talk about their emotions?

  - Are children encouraged to notice and understand the thoughts in their minds and how these thoughts can be linked to their emotions and behaviour?

  - What opportunities do all children have to practise healthy coping skills and problem-solving strategies? *Think about learning how to get along with others, how to handle challenge and failure, and how to resolve conflict.*

- How do staff work together to promote children's resilience? – Use the information in Chapter 2 to think in terms of:

  - **I have** – the things that are available in the school environment
  - **I am** – the characteristics and traits that make individuals who they are
  - **I can** – the things children can do (or learn to do) with the support of others.

- Are extracurricular activities valued and promoted in school as a way of helping children to connect with each other, achieve, and develop positive self-esteem and social skills?

- Do staff view behavioural incidents as opportunities to teach about emotions and feelings, and value the importance of a relational framework for managing behaviour?

- How does your school encourage peer support through, for example, peer mentoring schemes, anti-bullying ambassadors and buddy systems?

3. Do policies reflect a whole school commitment to positive mental health?

- Think about the current policies that relate, or should relate, to mental health. Which ones might you need to develop? Think in terms of pastoral care, managing bereavement and loss, promoting and managing positive mental health, identifying and supporting mental health problems, behaviour management and the continual professional development needs of the staff.

Reflection points for 'targeted' mental health matters

1. Do staff in school know how to identify and support emerging mental health problems in children?

- Does everyone have a good understanding of child development so they know what positive mental health looks like and how to spot early warning signs of emerging problems?
- Are all staff familiar with the factors that can place children at increased risk of mental health problems?
- Do all staff understand that behaviour, both externalising, challenging behaviour as well as internalising, withdrawn behaviour, can be a sign of an unmet mental health need?
- Is there a range of one-to-one and group interventions for children with emerging mental health needs?
- Are there clear systems for monitoring the emotional well-being of children, and measuring the impact of interventions when there are emerging mental health concerns?

2. Are there targeted interventions for children who are experiencing mental health difficulties?

- Do staff have good links with specialist staff and external agencies to seek advice, plan and implement targeted interventions, and make appropriate and timely referrals for children with identified needs?
- How are targeted interventions monitored and how is progress measured?
- Can children access individual counselling support in school, or locally?

- Are all staff clear about the referral systems and support pathways available locally for children with mental health difficulties?
- How do you review the continuing professional development needs of all school staff regarding targeted mental health identification and support?

Mental health awareness and care is a vital life skill, and by prioritising it in school we acknowledge the importance of mental health education as a universal offer for all children. By ensuring that all children have access to mental health information and opportunities to learn how to understand and care for their minds, we can hopefully prevent some mental health problems from escalating into more challenging difficulties. However, good universal mental health education will also support the effective and timely identification of children who may need additional targeted support.

Being aware of our mental health and how to manage it is beneficial for everyone in school – including adults! As we noted in Chapter 1, we all have mental health – so let's start talking about it.

Let's make mental health matter!

Bibliography

Akerman, R. and Statham, J. (2014), 'Bereavement in childhood: the impact on psychological and educational outcomes and the effectiveness of support services', Childhood Wellbeing Research Centre [www.cwrc.ac.uk/news/documents/Revised_Childhood_Bereavement_review_2014a.pdf]

Allen, M., Institute of Health Equity (2014), 'Local action on health inequalities: Building children and young people's resilience in schools', Public Health England

Anti-bullying alliance (2013), 'Reducing the incidence and impact of bullying for children and young people with SEND, Young people's views on bullying and mental health', DfE [www.anti-bullyingalliance.org.uk/media/5439/Mental-health-and-bullying-views-of-young-people-report.pdf]

Bomber, L. (2008), *Inside I'm hurting*, Worth Publishing

Child bereavement UK, *Schools* www.childbereavementuk.org/support/schools

Clement, S. et al (2014), 'What is the impact of mental health-related stigma on help-seeking? A systematic review of quantitative and qualitative studies', in *Psychological Medicine*, Cambridge University Press [http://cahealthequity.org/wp-content/uploads/2014/02/Impact-of-mental-health-related-stigma.pdf]

DfE (2015), 'Mental health and behaviour in schools, departmental advice for school staff', Crown copyright [www.gov.uk/government/uploads/system/uploads/attachment_data/file/416786/Mental_Health_and_Behaviour_-_Information_and_Tools_for_Schools_240515.pdf]

DfE (2014), 'Press release: Mental health behaviour guidance to be issued to schools' [www.gov.uk/government/news/mental-health-behaviour-guidance-to-be-issued-to-schools]

DfE (2015), 'Promoting the health and well-being of looked after children: Statuory guidance for local authorities, clinical commissioning groups and NHS England', Crown Copyright [www.gov.uk/government/uploads/system/uploads/attachment_data/file/413368/Promoting_the_health_and_well-being_of_looked-after_children.pdf]

DfE (2015), 'Special Educational Needs and Disability Code of Practice: 0 to 25 years', Crown Copyright [www.gov.uk/government/uploads/system/uploads/attachment_data/file/398815/SEND_Code_of_Practice_January_2015.pdf]

Emerson, E. and Hatton, C. (2007), 'The mental health of children and adolescents with learning disabilities in Britain', Lancaster University [www.lancaster.ac.uk/staff/emersone/FASSWeb/Emerson_07_FPLD_MentalHealth.pdf]

Gray, C. (1994), *Comic Strip Conversations: Illustrated interactions that Teach Conversation Skills to Students with Autism and Related Disorders*, Future Horizons

Gray, C. (1994, rev. 2010), *The New Social Story™ Book*, Future Horizons

Green, H. et al (2004), 'Mental health of children and young people in Great Britain, 2004 Summary report', Office for National Statistics, Crown copyright [www.hscic.gov.uk/catalogue/PUB06116/ment-heal-chil-youn-peop-gb-2004-rep2.pdf]

Grotberg, E. (1995), 'A guide to promoting resilience in children: strengthening the human spirit', *Early Childhood Development: Practice and Reflections Number 8,* Bernard Van Leer Foundation. [www.bernardvanleer.org/A_guide_to_promoting_resilience_in_children_ Strengthening_the_human_spirit]

Hébert, T. P. (1999), 'Culturally diverse high-achieving students in an urban high school', Urban education

Krug, E.G. et al (2002), 'The world report on violence and health', The Lancet Vol. 360 [www. ayamm.org/english/Violence%20against%20women%204.pdf]

Layard, R. et al (2013), 'What predicts a successful life? A life-course model of well-being', Centre for economic performance [http://cep.lse.ac.uk/pubs/download/dp1245.pdf]

Leavey, G. et al, Barnet, Enfield and Haringey Mental Health Trust (2005), 'Identification and management of pupils with mental health difficulties: a study of UK teachers' experience and views', NASUWT [www.researchgate.net/publication/260942763_Identification_and_ Management_of_Pupils_with_Mental_Health_Difficulties]

Madders, T. (2010), 'You need to know', National Autistic Society

Mind, 'Mental health facts and statistics' [www.mind.org.uk/information-support/types-of-mental-health-problems/statistics-and-facts-about-mental-health/how-common-are-mental-health-problems/]

National Institute for Health and Care Excellence (NICE) clinical guideline (2013), 'Antisocial behaviour and conduct disorders in children and young people: recognition and management', NICE [www.nice.org.uk/guidance/cg158/resources/antisocial-behaviour-and-conduct-disorders-in-children-and-young-people-recognition-and-management-35109638019781]

National Institute for Health and Care Excellence (NICE) (2013), 'Children's attachment guidelines: Final scope', NICE www.nice.org.uk/guidance/gid-cgwave0675/resources/childrens-attachment-final-scope2

Newton, C., Taylor, G. and Wilon, D. (1996), 'Circles of friends. An inclusive approach to meeting emotional and behavioural difficulties', Educational Psychology in Practice 11 41–48

Populus (2014), 'Survey to gauge the level of knowledge and awareness of child and adolescent mental health' [www.rcpch.ac.uk/news/thousands-young-people-risk-'slipping-through-net'-due-adults'-lack-mental-health-awareness]

Royal College of Psychiatrists (2010), 'No health without public mental health: the case for action' [www.rcpsych.ac.uk/pdf/Position%20Statement%204%20website.pdf]

Royal College of Psychiatrists (2005), 'Depression in children and young people: Factsheet for young people' www.rcpsych.ac.uk/healthadvice/parentsandyouthinfo/youngpeople/depressioninyoungpeople.aspx

Sempik, J., Ward, H. and Darker, I. (2008), 'Emotional and behavioural difficulties of children and young people at entry into care', Clinical child psychology and psychiatry 13(2) 221–233

Shotton, G. (1998), 'A circle of friends approach for socially neglected children', Educational Psychology in Practice 14 issue 1 22–25

St John, T. et al (2004), 'Childhood and Adolescent Mental Health: understanding the lifetime impacts', Mental Health Foundation [http://www.mentalhealth.org.uk/content/assets/PDF/publications/lifetime_impacts.pdf]

Stalker, D. 'Start young, stay active: Childhood physical literacy report', UK active [www.ukactive. com/downloads/managed/Start_Young_Stay_Active.pdf]

Taylor, S., Hart, A. and Hove Park School, 'The resilient classroom: A resource pack for tutor groups and pastoral school staff, BOND and YoungMinds [www.youngminds.org.uk/ assets/0001/1548/The_resilient_classroom.pdf]

TNS BMRB (2015), 'Attitudes to mental illness 2014 research report', TNS BMRB [https://www. time-to-change.org.uk/sites/default/files/Attitudes_to_mental_illness_2014_report_ final_0.pdf]

Weare, K. (2015), 'What works in promoting social and emotional well-being and responding to mental health problems in schools?', National Children's Bureau [www.ncb.org.uk/ media/1197143/ncb_framework_for_promoting_well-being_and_responding_to_ mental_health_in_schools.pdf]

Index